CORRECTING TREATMENT IN CORRECTIONS

Rhonda L. Champagne
Michael B. Johnson

The events and conversations in this book have been set down to the best of the authors' abilities. Some names and details have been changed to protect the privacy of individuals.

All events described herein actually happened, though on occasion, the authors have taken certain, very small, liberties with chronology.

First paperback edition (month) 2020

Book design by Rhonda Champagne & Michael Johnson

ISBN 978-1-09834-364-4 (Paperback)
ISBN 978-1-09834-397-2 (Hardback)
ISBN 978-1-09834-365-1 (eBook)

Published by

Rhonda Champagne and Michael Johnson

Edited by

Ersula Butler for YUVA Business & Writing Services

You write in order to change the world, knowing perfectly well that you probably can't, but also knowing that literature is indispensable to the world...

The world changes according to the way people see it, and if you alter, even by a millimeter, the way... people look at reality, then you can change it[1]

James Baldwin

1 Pipher, Mary. (2006). *Writing to Change the World.* Riverhead Books

CONTENTS

PREFACE

Michael Johnson / Rhonda Champagne

> ***"The United States is the world's leader in incarceration with 2.2 million people currently in the nation's prisons and jails, a 500 percent increase over the last forty years. Changes in sentencing law and policy, not changes in crime rates, explain most of this increase. These trends have resulted in prison overcrowding and fiscal burdens on states to accommodate a rapidly expanding penal system, despite increasing evidence that large scale incarceration is not an effective means of achieving public safety."***[2]

It is time we seriously debate and challenge our current process of ensuring community safety, while at the same time, addressing the underlining causes of criminal behavior. It's time to seriously question the effects of power and control over incarcerated people versus understanding and treating human behavior. Is power and control making our communities safer, or would understanding and treating human behavior better support public safety?

Over the last 40 years, incarceration rates in the United States have almost doubled as a result of our justice system and its guidelines. Statistics

---

2 The Sentencing Project. (2017). *Research and Advocacy and Reform* www. Sentencingproject.org/criminal-justice-facts/

suggest that this approach to the problem has only increased incarceration levels.

Montana's top ten criminal offenses for both male and female offenders make up the majority of the prison inmate population.

Montana Top 10 Criminal Offenses for Male and Female Offenders[3]

Males

1. Criminal Possession of Dangerous Drugs
2. Criminal Endangerment
3. Theft
4. Felony DUI
5. Burglary
6. Assault with a Weapon
7. Partner Family Member Assault
8. Criminal Possession with Intent to Distribute
9. Criminal Distribution of Drugs
10. Failure to Register

Females

1. Criminal Possession of Dangerous Drugs
2. Criminal Endangerment
3. Theft
4. Felony DUI
5. Criminal Distribution of Drugs
6. Criminal Child Endangerment
7. Forgery

3 Top Ten Offenses for Male and Female Offenders in Montana (2019). https://cor.mt.gov/Portals/104/Resources/Reports/2019biennialreport.pdf

8. Criminal Possession with Intent to Distribute
9. Burglary
10. Bail Jumping

What we don't see on the top ten list of crimes is murder and sex crimes, such as child molestation. Most of the top ten crimes are related to addiction. Studies suggest many addictions are related to underlining trauma. Addiction and trauma can be treated.

The correctional systems across the United States of America have a goal to reduce recidivism through treatment. In this book, the authors challenge how treatment is being implemented within the correctional system. Are security policies and procedures supporting a treatment environment? This is a difficult ethical topic to debate. Arguments can be, and have been, made to uphold opposing positions. This book is intended to further discussion and debate on how to best ensure public safety, reduce overcrowding prisons, reduce costs, reduce recidivism, support victims, and at the same time, provide successful trauma and addiction treatment for offenders.

The authors share their rollercoaster ride of emotions and the challenges they faced while creating and implementing a trauma treatment program within a correctional facility. Throughout the process, they struggled with the mandated policies and procedures that often seemed more appropriate for a maximum-level security setting. The reader will follow Rhonda Champagne, a trauma therapist, as she enters the shocking world of corrections, from a treatment perspective. The reader will also follow Lieutenant Michael Johnson's challenges to uphold safety and security measures while moving into the unfamiliar world of treatment. They quickly found the two worlds to be counteractive and counterproductive in many ways. The program and treatment philosophies that were implemented over months stretched the bounds of both conventional treatment and a conventional correctional environment.

Their journey was filled with extreme stress, hilarious episodes, unique characters, and a great deal of psychological and philosophical challenges. During this journey, they both experienced laughter, happiness, sadness, anger, frustration, tears, gratitude, resentment, and every other emotion known to humans. It was a unique experience with special people involved in its functioning. From the corrections staff who worked there, to the women who arrived for treatment, all experienced a level of connectedness not typically found in a correctional setting. Truly, a level of magic took hold of this group of people, the processes and the program's purpose.

This is the story of the Riverside Recovery and Reentry Program, a trauma rehabilitation pilot program for incarcerated women from prisons or jails across Montana. The program was developed in the Fall of 2015, in a secured prison facility, previously used to house juvenile girls. The facility sat on approximately five acres of fenced-in land located just outside the small town of Boulder, Montana. The chain link fence stood approximately twenty feet high and included three rows of barb wire across the top. Within the fence line were five separate brick buildings. The housing unit was divided into east and west units. Each had its own dayroom, eating area, and hall of bedrooms. There were 14 bedrooms in total, and 32 beds. Some bedrooms had only one bed, some had two beds and others contained three beds. Kitchen and laundry areas were shared by both units. Two security offices provided a full spectrum observation of the dayrooms.

As a result of an increase in community-based programs for juveniles, the Riverside facility became available for a Montana Department of Corrections (DOC) pilot program that was to be designed to treat the underlying trauma that so many incarcerated people have experienced. The pilot program had stunning positive results. Despite significant controversy, often uncomfortable dialog, and sometimes wrenching compromises, it became a place of healing and hope. This is a story of two seemingly opposing worlds ultimately coming together to create a successful trauma-informed treatment environment for offenders, without compromising safety and security requirements.

We invite you, the reader, to arrive at your own conclusion as how to best implement treatment in a secure setting without further traumatizing the people being treated.

ACKNOWLEDGEMENTS

Michael Johnson / Rhonda Champagne

We would like to thank every person who has the compassion to see people for who they can be, as opposed to what they've done. We thank the people who understand how a person's behavior can be greatly impacted by the environment in which they are in.

We would also like to thank every person who has the courage to question, and ultimately revise, any process being implemented primarily because, "That's the way we've always done it."

In the case of Riverside, a true treatment facility was created, implemented, and ultimately became a psychologically and physically safe healing program. Many of the residents and staff have healed in varying degrees.

We thank the Montana Department of Corrections (DOC) for allowing this program to exist. And we thank the 189 women who entered the program and having the courage to heal. We thank everyone who believed in and implemented a perfect balance of law, ethics, policy, guidelines, and compassion that supported a safe and secure treatment environment and culture.

We would like to thank the people who supported us and were dedicated and resourceful in helping us through the process of writing this book.

Ersula Butler, thank you for your final edits. Susan Woodrow, thank you for your content and flow editing. Theresa Scott, thank you for correcting our grammar and line-by-line editing. Matt Wilson, thank you for your review and feedback. Dee Dee Antis, thank you for the many reads, input and support. Janelle Lafser, your support and encouragement was truly invaluable during this process. Matt Hoffman, your read and invaluable feedback has been tremendously helpful. And to Steven Bates at Helena Print and Design, thank you for the book cover work.

To all our family and friends, thank you for listening and supporting us throughout the two-year process. We could not have stuck with it without your support.

INTRODUCTION

Michael Johnson, 'The Lieutenant'

My name is Michael Johnson. My career in corrections has spanned nearly fourteen years, twelve of those with the Montana Department of Corrections (DOC). I retired in early 2020 from the DOC as a lieutenant. My corrections experience broadly includes working with juvenile boys and girls, and adult men and women. I have worked with incarcerated people in a correctional setting of both genders, ranging in age from 13 to 90 years old.

I do not represent or speak for the DOC. I am writing from my own perspective, experience and opinion. I reference the Montana DOC only to share my experiences and to share how my beliefs have evolved over time.

I loved my career in corrections. I enjoyed working with people, especially those who have made poor, and even terrible choices. I value corrections work. I was, and still am, honored and proud of my service. However, my experiences did not come without some lingering regrets.

I had held different professional titles throughout the program and population transitions at my facility. When I first began employment, the housing unit staff held the titles of correctional counselor, shift supervisor and unit supervisor. These titles that translated into military rank, are correctional officer, sergeant and lieutenant. Military rank titles were not used at my facility when working with the youth population, or with the trauma treatment program. The housing unit staff conducted basic life skills groups and individual basic counseling. However, we were not certified counselors. The DOC did not offer training specific to the correctional counselor role, instead we were sent to Correctional Detention Officer (CDO) Basic Course training. This is a 4-week long training mandated for all county jail and state prison officers. As correctional counselors, we were issued an officer's badge by the DOC, but the facility would not allow us to hold or wear the badge. The superintendent was concerned the badge would interfere with the relationship-based rapport between housing unit staff and the incarcerated population.

In the first two chapters, I refer to all housing unit staff by their military rank. This title will best identify the security trainings we received, and the responsibilities expected of us. In chapter four, they will be referred to as correctional counselors, to describe the transformation that took place.

INTRODUCTION

Rhonda Champagne, 'The Therapist'

My name is Rhonda Champagne. I am a licensed clinical social worker, a therapist. I graduated with a master's degree from Walla Walla University. I currently work in a private practice. I was hired by the Montana DOC to assist with the implementation of a pilot trauma-informed treatment program for adult female inmates, or as I prefer to call them, women. I worked most of my college and post-college career in a community mental healthcare center where I wore many hats, each one for about 3 years including day treatment specialist, case manager, crisis intervention specialist, therapist, team leader, and eventually the director. I helped serve over 1,700 people suffering from a wide range of serious and disabling mental illnesses. My heart and soul lived there. I have worked with doctors and lawyers, receptionists and janitors. I have worked with people heading to prison and people leaving prison. I have testified on their behalf and against them. I have diagnosed and treated, bathed and fed, but where I made the most impact, and felt the best about myself, was when I *connected and related with* people.

My personal history helps me connect with people. I connect with those who grew up without a father presence. I connect with those who had developed differently. My 'sister-aunt' had Downs Syndrome and she helped me to relate to people different than myself. I also relate to bullying and being bullied. As a product of generational poverty, I am able to relate with the needs and desires that push desperate people to take desperate action that may leave one thinking, 'I must not be worthy.' I am part Native American, and so I relate with the effects of racism. I am female, and thus relate with sexism. I am the mother of a veteran incarcerated after desperately trying to outrun his trauma. I have had my own trauma too. I had to acknowledge it, clear it, and make peace with it before I could ultimately let it go. I'd much rather look at the gifts it provided me.

I love people who love others. And I love people who learn to love themselves. I particularly love people who learn to love themselves, even when it seems that others don't.

No matter where a person finds his or herself on the path of life, something miraculous happens when he or she begins to like who they are. I want to impact the correctional system to provide an environment where those who are sent for treatment can start to honestly forgive themselves and begin to like who they are.

A CAUTION TO THE READER

We want to caution our readers that some of the material in this book will describe details of trauma. This information could trigger trauma in the reader. The personal stories are disturbing, in many ways. Disturbing that any person would have to endure such events as told in this book. Disturbing to know people can inflict such trauma on another human being. Disturbing that much trauma is buried and lingers on, haunting the minds and interfering with the much-needed sleep of so many. We tried to leave the graphic details out. We trust that you, as the reader, know yourself best and will heed our caution if necessary.

I THOUGHT I WAS SAFE

Actual writing assignment to process a trauma event.
Resident Testimony

I made a few mistakes and broke the law. I was irresponsible and careless, and I got caught. I went to jail. I admitted to my wrongs, took accountability for my crimes. I was offered a dream come true, help for my trauma and abuse.

My most recent traumatic experience happened while incarcerated and under the "safe" care of the DOC. As an inmate, I thought I was protected. I thought in no way would the bad things of my past be repeated. The "law" would never let anything bad or harmful happen to me. They would "protect and serve," right?

Before I was to report to the trauma treatment facility, I was taken to a chemical dependency treatment facility located directly across the street from the trauma program. I had to wait five days before a bed was available before I could go to the trauma treatment I so looked forward to and desperately needed. The transport people left, and the security staff began the process of intake. I'd never been to a treatment place before. I was a little anxious, but these people seemed friendly enough, what would I have to fear?

The process began simply enough. Shackles off, lots of questions and places to sign. Next, a towel rested on my shoulders and some liquid that looked like industrial strength wood glue, only runnier, was put in my hair. Apparently, it was a lice-killing liquid. I didn't have lice, but she said, "everyone gets it." They don't want lice and a lot of people from county jails have lice. Again, I was grateful, better safe than sorry.

Next came the instructions for the strip search that was required that I was about to endure. The instructions were to go into the bathroom and stand behind the chair, so I was not seen on the security camera. I was directed to slowly take off and shake out each item of clothing. Then I was supposed to lift my breasts, shake out my hair, and show them behind my ears. The next step would be to reach down and grab my labia, spread it open, and squat. Then I was supposed to turn around, bend over, reach behind myself and open my butt cheeks, squat, and cough hard three times. All of this was, of course, to happen while this stranger I just met would be staring at me. This idea made me very uncomfortable. I explained how I mentally would not be able to do the things she was asking me to do. Something along the lines of, "it's policy" was her reply. My fears and feelings were being minimized and brushed off as if they were invalid.

For my entire life, I have had to perform acts that have made me feel uneasy and dirty. Now, with people I assumed would always keep me safe, contracted employees of DOC, my trauma was being triggered and I was forced to re-live my past trauma and abuse. I felt helpless. I saw no hope. I dragged my feet as emotions ran wild as I entered the bathroom. I was sweaty. My hands were clammy, but I was more afraid of being in trouble, so I reached for the bottom of my shirt. I clung to it and began to shift from side to side and plead with this person. Again, my feelings didn't matter to them.

I managed to finally get my shirt and bra off. Covering my nipples, I lifted my breasts. Next, I took off my pants. By this time, tears were pouring out of me. I pled some more as I showed her behind my ears and shook out my hair, all the while attempting to cover my breasts that were still exposed. I felt like I was backed into a corner. My only escape would be through this woman, and even if I was able to get through her, the door was locked. I was outnumbered and now only in my partially see-through, disposable panties from jail. I was shaking uncontrollably, crying, hyperventilating, and afraid. I was trapped. I knew from my past that the only way to make a bad person stop hurting me was to do whatever they wanted. I didn't know what they might do to me if I didn't do what they asked, but my past experiences told me it wouldn't be good. I reached for my panties, slipping my fingers in each side. Quickly, I yanked them back. I tried to compromise, asking if I could hold the hand towel in front of me and jump or bounce around to show her that there was nothing inside me. Again, I received an explanation leaving me feeling insignificant, confused, and alone. I couldn't yell for help. I couldn't run away.

As I reached for my panties a few more times, still unable to please this cruel audience, I began to feel empty. Something started to happen. I began to disconnect from reality. I tried to use the coping skill I had developed growing up. I was terrified and miserable. I was shutting down. I was lost and began to turn off who I was. I had to imagine I was somewhere else, as if I left my body and I wasn't really there. This helped a tiny bit, but reality abruptly came back to me. I was standing there mortified and extremely vulnerable, holding the hand towel in a desperate attempt to maintain some dignity. I can only describe what happened as feeling asleep and dreaming. I am somewhere else, doing something else, only to wake up in the middle of a nightmare.

The anxiety was unbearable. The anguish I was suffering from this degrading ordeal was only the beginning. I would still be forced to touch myself in front of this person. I was still supposed to grab down there and open it for someone to look at. I don't even look at it. Now, I must let someone else inspect my private parts? If I didn't, there would be consequences. I felt icky and wrong.

I don't understand why it's always the people who are supposed to keep me safe, the people who I trust, that hurt me the most. Even now, as I write the details of that day, I am shaking. I can't breathe, tears and fears are building up. I must end this story. I must walk away. It's just too much for me to bear. I don't want to go through it again. I can't. I am not okay.

CHAPTER ONE

Conflicting Cultures
Safety and Security vs. Treatment

Within the first week of the therapist being hired, she entered the lieutenant's office in the housing unit. The lieutenant's office was separate from the office that the security officers shared, but similarly, it had a wall of windows which provided a full view of the east dayroom. The second window portrayed a view of the Elk Horn mountain range through the security fence. The office was small, containing only a desk with a computer, and three additional chairs used primarily for disciplinary sessions. The therapist sat in one of these chairs and introduced herself. The lieutenant wasted little time before getting right to his point.

> ***Lieutenant:*** "I need you to understand the importance of having structure and control over the population in a correctional facility. If I don't keep a population busy and structured, they will keep us busy. In other words, if they aren't held to a strict schedule and program expectations, they will start acting out on each other, or on the staff. A large part of keeping a correctional facility safe and secure is to maintain structure and control over the population."

> ***Therapist:*** "I need you to understand the importance of self-direction in a treatment facility. Power and control are effective

only if the power and control continue to exist. If we are running a prison, then go for it. If you hold power over someone, they will comply unless they feel they've had enough. However, it has a potential to back-fire at times. This is not a prison, it's a treatment program and we need to allow everyone to come to their own direction in order to really integrate treatment."

Lieutenant: "We are providing treatment in a correctional facility to a population of inmates. Many of them have a history of being violent and manipulative. We need to acknowledge this, and I feel responsible for the safety of all staff, as well as inmates."

Therapist: "We need to refer to the women in this facility as residents. If we continue to see the person for what they've done, and continue to treat them as 'a violent person' or 'manipulative,' or an 'inmate,' we won't be providing treatment. How far do you think treatment will go? If you legitimately went to your doctor complaining of a headache or backache and the first thing your doctor did was to say to you, "stop manipulating me for pain pills," how likely are you to feel that you received treatment?"

Lieutenant: "What if I was, in fact, manipulating the doctor for pain pills, but the doctor unknowingly or unwillingly, neglected to look at my history of medication seeking, resulting in the doctor subscribing the pain pills? Then, what if I overdose on the pills? Or worse, hurt someone else due to my misuse of the medication? What happens to that doctor's license to practice?"

Therapist: "Would you please answer my questions rather than try to run me down a rabbit hole? Honestly, how would you feel about the treatment you received from your doctor? This is a treatment facility, not a prison."

Lieutenant: "First of all, I am not taking you down a rabbit hole. You started the doctor analogy. The rabbit hole is yours, not mine. With that being said, I do see your point. If I was legitimately injured, and the doctor assumed I was being manipulative and therefore did not treat me for my injury, I would be upset, to say the least. In addition, I see the connection you are making to the level of treatment we would be providing if we treat people like they are their worst-case scenario. But how, then, do we trust the person who is seeking treatment, and how do we identify a dangerous or manipulative person? Now, can you answer the questions which I've asked you?"

Therapist: "I see your point that the doctor could be held liable. However, I believe we should provide a blanket of trust, while at the same time, demonstrating that trust by acknowledging the humanness of every female being treated in this facility. I believe if there are dangerous or manipulative people here, they will identify themselves through their behavior."

Lieutenant: "You are killing me. Are you saying we just wait for the effects of the danger or manipulation to present itself, and then we respond? All my training instills the need to prevent danger and manipulation. When a person becomes a danger or is manipulating the treatment program, the consequence should be the removal from the program, as quickly as possible. This will send a message to the rest of the population that we will not tolerate dangerous behavior or manipulation."

Therapist: "If we are transparent up front, and thoroughly explain that we do not tolerate abuse, violence or manipulation, we must also explain the direct consequences of such behavior. I think we can enforce the same consequences for someone not willing to engage in treatment. If we can properly communicate this to the residents, I would be more likely to agree with you."

Lieutenant: "I agree. We need clear communication of the expectations and consequences. My officers will also appreciate these clear directives in managing the population and program expectations."

Substance Abuse and Mental Health Services Administration© (SAMHSA)

As the pilot project was to be a Substance Abuse and Mental Health Treatment program, the therapist turned to the key principles of a trauma informed approach, as published by Substance Abuse and Mental Health Services Administration (SAMHSA)©.[4] Having prior experience with these guidelines and knowing the resources and stakeholders needed to implement best practices, she turned to SAMHSA©. She printed out the Six Key Principles of a Trauma-Informed Approach and 12 bullet points on recovery culture, and then asked the lieutenant to review the information and implement their use as a daily tool.

SAMHSA's Six Key Principles of a Trauma-Informed Approach[5]

- **Safety:** Both staff and clients must feel safe physically and psychologically.
- **Peer Support:** Can help foster hope, build trust, and enhance collaboration.
- **Trustworthiness & Transparency:** A trauma-informed care setting will emphasize building honest and open relationships.
- **Collaboration & Mutuality:** A leveling of power between staff and clients.

4 Substance Abuse and Mental Health Services Administration (SAMHSA)© https://www.samhsa.gov

5 Ibid.

- **Cultural, Historical, and Gender Issues:** Can be used as strengths that will facilitate healing and growth.
- **Empowerment voice and choice:** All individuals' strengths and experiences are recognized and built upon.

Therapist: "Let's go over the guidelines. Safety is most important, both staff and clients must feel safe physically and psychologically."

Lieutenant: "My highest priority is the safety of all staff and inmates. Our policies and procedures are created to maintain the safety of everyone."

Therapist: "Also, we need to implement peer support processes and enhance collaboration. It fosters hope."

Lieutenant: "We can encourage inmates to support each other throughout their program."

Therapist: "We need to have trustworthiness and transparency by building honest and open relationships between staff and residents."

Lieutenant: "Honesty won't be a problem, but I'm not entirely sure I understand what you mean by open relationships between officers and inmates. We have strict policies on professional boundaries with inmates. These policies will be followed."

Therapist: "We also need to acknowledge cultural, historical, and gender issues as they become strengths that will facilitate healing and growth. *All* residents' strengths and experiences should be recognized and built upon."

Lieutenant: "This sounds good in theory and I would assume this will be implemented in the treatment curriculum. I don't see how this will conflict with the safety and security requirements."

Therapist: "We also need to empower the women and make sure they have a voice and choice in as many ways as we can."

Lieutenant: "This is a correctional facility. They have the choice to comply with the rules and expectations. If they don't comply, there will be written incident reports and appropriate sanctions. When they want to have a voice, they can fill out a 'request to speak to staff' form."

Therapist: "A request to speak to staff form? Are you kidding? Think about that and tell me how that offers any empowerment? These women are products of relationships that were as dominating as you are demonstrating right now! They need to experience making choices and know that they don't have to follow someone else's direction, especially when that direction is purely based on power, simply because someone happens to have power over them."

Lieutenant: "I'm not saying they don't have a voice. I'm only saying there needs to be order in the way they communicate with officers. They can't be stopping the officers every second when they want to make a complaint or tell us how we should be running the program. And they will! There needs to be order. Do you know what it's like to walk on a unit and have ten inmates, all at the same time, bombing you with complaints and requests? I do. It's unmanageable. If they want to talk to an officer, they need to fill out a request form."

Therapist: "I don't know what it is like to be on the unit. Can we agree to be open to finding a way to implement this guideline in the future? On some level?

Lieutenant: "No. the request forms will be used."

Therapist: "These guidelines will need to be structured in all areas of the program, including outside of the treatment curriculum, especially the housing unit because that is where the residents will spend most of their time. Collaboration and mutuality are primary as it levels the power between staff and clients."

Lieutenant: "You want me to 'level the power' between inmates and officers?"

Therapist: "Yes."

Lieutenant: "No."

Therapist: "Why not?"

Lieutenant: "Because we are a correctional facility. We keep people safe by controlling and managing inmates. The officers are the authority figures and they will maintain their role as such. Safety is the first principle listed on your SAMSHA© guidelines and it is the primary objective for the DOC."

Therapist: "We are a treatment program. You can help them feel psychologically safe by not sanctioning them for having an extra sugar packet or dryer sheet."

Lieutenant: "How does managing the use of items such as sugar packets and dryer sheets have anything to do with 'leveling of power' between inmates and officers? I am referring to the authority officers will have over inmates to ensure the safety of all inmates and staff. We will have rules in place which ensure officers have control over the facility and inmates. This is necessary for the safety and security of all who work here. Regarding your issue with me managing sugar packets and dryer sheets, do you know who pays for those sugar packets and dryer sheets?"

Therapist: "Issuing sanctions for having an extra sugar packet exerts unnecessary power. I understand the need to be conscientious about spending, but there are other ways to assure reducing waste besides issuing consequences. Sanctions threaten the psychological safety of the residents."

Lieutenant: "The taxpayer pays for everything we issue to the inmates. In one way or another, it is the taxpayer's money. I manage everything the inmates use because if I don't, every inmate uses twice of what they need. When I don't manage these things, the taxpayer pays double. If there are not consequences for using excess items, how can I control excess spending?"

Therapist: "Well, I would like to try to address these things in therapy and use them as a learning tool to get the women to see the perspective of the taxpayer and come to their own conclusion, prior to getting a write up."

Lieutenant: "In a correctional setting we inform inmates of the rules and the consequences of breaking those rules. When they break a rule, we follow through with a consequence. This prepares them to be accountable for their actions and accept the consequences of breaking laws."

Therapist: "That may work in a prison, but in a treatment program, it does not offer a leveling of power. It threatens, which creates an extreme set of emotions that do not provide psychological safety. It sets a stage and is a constant reminder that they are being controlled, rather than self-empowered."

Lieutenant: "A leveling of power will be difficult to implement in a correctional facility. Look.... I care about these inmates. I want to see them succeed and become successful members of our communities. I want to support whatever is needed for them to overcome their weaknesses. However, I will not lose control of the housing unit. If this happens, people will get hurt. It could be the inmates, or it could be a staff member. It is imperative that I maintain control. These inmates must know that if they jeopardize the safety of the unit, I will not tolerate it. It feels like you are pushing me to surrender that influence over the unit and this population. That will prove to be dangerous for people, and I will not allow it."

Therapist: "I truly am not pushing you to surrender the safety of everyone on the unit. Let's agree to table this conversation, as you suggested, for another day.

Strip Search Debate

The superintendent called for the first planning meeting. In attendance were the superintendent, compliance specialist, housing manager (LT), trauma therapist (LCSW), chemical dependency counselor, case manager, medical nurse (RN), and fitness teacher.

The superintendent began the meeting by informing the team that research-based studies show that most incarcerated women have underlining trauma which greatly influences addiction and criminal behavior. The DOC assigned the Riverside team to create and implement a pilot program designed to provide trauma treatment to an adult female population, incarcerated within the prison and or jail system of Montana. "The first item on today's agenda is the intake process." He informed us that the inmates would first complete an application to participate in the program. The treatment team would then review applications for placement. Inmates would arrive by transport in full restraints and, after removing the restraints, each one would be escorted to a secure, private area where a female officer would conduct an "unclothed search."

Therapist: "Wait a minute, wait a minute. What is an unclothed search? Is that a strip search?"

Lieutenant: "The unclothed search is the same process as a strip search, although, it is not called a strip search anymore because that phrase is offensive."

Therapist: "Calling a strip search an unclothed search does not make the process any less offensive. We cannot have strip searches or unclothed searches in a treatment program. What is the need for an unclothed search when they first arrive? My understanding is that these women are arriving from incarceration in a jail or prison, and they have been strip searched in those facilities. Why would we do it again?"

Lieutenant: "We absolutely need to have unclothed searches upon intake, as well as after contact visits, and any other time we deem it necessary to ensure the safety and security of the facility, staff, and other inmates. We know there are drugs in prisons and in county jails. We know inmates successfully hide not only drugs, but also weapons, which are not always found in unclothed searches. We don't know if the unclothed searches in the other facilities were conducted thoroughly or properly. We don't know if an inmate may have managed to pick up contraband during the transport. We need to conduct unclothed searches at intake to be confident inmates are not entering our facility with any contraband. This is for the safety and security of all who work here as well as the other inmates."

Therapist: "What is contraband?"

Lieutenant: "Contraband is anything an inmate is not authorized to have, or anything they are approved to have, but are using it for something other than what it was intended to be used for."

Therapist: "That's clear as mud. These women are coming into a treatment program, not a prison. What about their safety?

How can you expect to provide treatment after strip searching them? This is a treatment program!"

Lieutenant: "How safe will it be when an inmate brings in a drug like crystal meth and then becomes violent and physically hurts another inmate or worse, a staff member? That staff could be you. We are a correctional facility!"

Therapist: "A treatment program requires psychological safety as well as physical safety. How can we state that we are providing treatment when the first thing you want to do is re-traumatize and demoralize them?"

Lieutenant: "I understand an unclothed search is not a pleasant experience, but my officers have had extensive training in conducting unclothed searches professionally, and with as little discomfort as possible."

Therapist: "We are targeting a female population who have a history of trauma. Most initial trauma experienced by females occurred by being molested or raped. I don't care how professionally or nicely you mandate a woman take her clothes off, spread open her labia, then squat and cough while spreading her buttocks apart. You will be introducing additional trauma. I'll have no part of that, especially as a therapist!"

Lieutenant: "As the therapist, you will not have to conduct the unclothed searches. I understand if you were to conduct an unclothed search, it could negatively influence your therapeutic relationship with the inmates. That is the job of the female officers. This is what officers in corrections do to ensure the safety and security of the facility."

Therapist: "It makes no difference to treatment whether I conduct the strip search, or your female officers conduct the strip search. The process of a strip search itself is not conducive to a treatment environment or culture. It is, in fact, detrimental to successful treatment, regardless of who conducts the strip search, and no matter how professionally you think the process can be done. All staff, including yourself, will need to build a therapeutic relationship with these women. Isn't there any other way to ensure the safety and security without the process of a strip search? Can't we get one of those body scanners like they use at airports?"

Lieutenant: "No, there isn't another way. We can't afford to buy a body scanner. This is what we do. It's the only way to keep people and the environment safe."

Therapist: "You stated that all kinds of contraband gets missed in a search. When was the last time you found contraband by strip searching someone?"

Lieutenant: "That's true. An unclothed search will not detect all contraband, but it will detect most contraband, and that is better than not conducting the search. We did, in fact, confiscate a crochet hook from a female offender through an unclothed search. The offender was attempting to dig her way through the ceiling of her cell using the hook. When we realized the hook was missing, the offender hid it in her vagina. Also, when inmates know we are conducting unclothed searches, that alone will often deter them from attempting to hide contraband in their body."

Therapist: "So, you found contraband through a strip search one time in the last decade?"

Lieutenant: "To my recollection, yes."

Therapist: "You've done hundreds, if not thousands, of strip searches and found one person with contraband and that is somehow supposed to make strip searching a reasonable method of finding contraband? How successful do you think chemical dependency treatment would be if it was mandated that every person start treatment by having a cocktail, then having another cocktail whenever they have a visit, and another cocktail whenever they were transported to the dentist, doctor, or a court hearing, etc.? This pilot project will not be a trauma treatment facility if it is required that each woman be re-traumatized every time they arrive, have a visit, or go to the dentist or doctor."

Lieutenant: "I've never conducted an unclothed search on a female offender and neither have any other male officers. Female officers are the only officers allowed to conduct an unclothed search. In order to ensure the safety and security of this facility, we need unclothed searches. They're absolutely necessary. I'll do everything in my power to keep inmates, my officers and you safe."

Therapist: "You seem to think sexual abuse and molestation are perpetrated only by men, but many children and adults have been abused by a person of the same sex. It's not about how respectful you can be during the process, it's about the process itself. If a civilian were to conduct a strip search, it would be considered a criminal act and would land the person in jail for a sexual abuse crime. Somehow, the correctional system considers it a professional procedure. It is barbaric, outdated, demoralizing, dehumanizing, traumatizing, and has no place in a treatment program! If we do even one strip search, I will not work here."

The Therapist Draws the Line

During a planning meeting, the therapist told the superintendent she would walk out of the facility if even one strip search was conducted. She didn't say this in a manner which would support a threat, or even as an unprofessional derogatory line of communication. Instead, it was delivered more as a clear line she could not cross, and she therefore felt it important to inform the superintendent that she would not be able to continue her employment if strip searches occurred. This would go against her professional and personal ethics and morals.

Her statement immediately stopped all conversation and debate around the table. For a split second, it was like being in an old western movie. The therapist was calling out the superintendent and challenging him to step across the line she had just drawn in the dirt street in front of the saloon. The rest of the staff held their breath as they looked at the superintendent to see if he would accept the challenge.

He didn't go there. In fact, he had the same blank look on his face as the rest of us. They watched as he processed the therapist's statement. He shifted around in his chair, trying to buy himself time as he compiled the best neutral, and uncommitted response he could come up with. It went something like this, 'Well, I'm not saying we will do an unclothed search, I'm only saying we need a policy in place detailing what the process will look like, if we ever had to do one.'

So, with that neutral and uncommitted answer, it became the therapist's turn to put on her blank face as she struggled to translate his answer. For everyone else around the table, his answer doubled down on the complexity and confusion in the conversation. Some people just tuned out completely and retreated to their safe place. Many superintendents in his position would have told the therapist to hit the road. Instead, he had the courage and willingness to entertain the possibility there could be a solution. This was just enough to keep the therapist employed and keep the strip search topic tabled until future planning meetings. Without him doing this, the story of Riverside would have ended right there.

The Therapist's Office

The superintendent told the therapist, "This is your office. We want you to decorate it anyway that makes you feel comfortable. Make it your home."

The next day, his eyes became very large as she continued to bring in things that made it comfortable, like her own home, like he said to do. The therapist wasn't ready for this world of corrections, and the expressions the staff had when they entered her office indicated they weren't ready for her treatment world. It wasn't until the lieutenant entered her office that she was given some direct communication as to what the concerns were. There was no shortage of sarcasm from either of them, but they managed to get through it with a degree of humor.

> ***Lieutenant:*** "Hello. I hear you have your office set up. Mind if I come in?"
>
> ***Therapist:*** "Sure, come on in. Have a seat if you want."
>
> ***Lieutenant:*** "Oh wow. This is an interesting set up. I see you got your new conference table. Is this where you are going to have your trauma groups with the inmates?"
>
> ***Therapist:*** "Yes, this is where I will hold trauma groups with the women. I would have preferred a round table, but an oval one is better than square; it helps with the leveling of power."
>
> ***Lieutenant:*** "The leveling of what....? Never mind, don't answer that. What's with this big ceramic bowl with all the ink pens in the middle of the table?"
>
> ***Therapist:*** "Well, the women will be doing a lot of writing and that bowl holds enough pens for all of them."

Lieutenant: "You can say that again.... The inmates can break that bowl over someone's head. As for the ink pens, there is enough there for at least two inmates to give themselves full body tattoos. We call this stuff contraband."

Therapist: "Well, I am absolutely positive I won't be hosting a tattoo party. It's called group therapy, and the tools I have will be used appropriately."

Lieutenant: "We'll see about that. Just make sure you let me know if a pen comes up missing. You should number them, so you'll know if one does come up missing. What's this on your desk?"

Therapist: "It's a crystal rock. Some crystals absorb negative energy. I think it'll be a useful tool for the women."

Lieutenant: "Wait a minute...You are going to hand this softball sized rock to the inmates when they are having negative feelings? Have you considered how they could throw it at you, or at another inmate, or just use it as brass knuckles and bash someone's face in?"

Therapist: "I highly doubt any woman in our treatment program will use it as a weapon to bash someone's face in as long as you aren't in the room."

Lieutenant: "Trust me..., this office is the last place I want to be with the inmates. What do we have over here...? Oh... nice, a four-foot giant glass vase with.... what are these sticks inside of it? The sticks will be fun for the inmates to whip each other with. There's enough here for everyone. I like how you have it positioned perfectly between these two wardrobe mirrors on the wall. If an inmate smashes these mirrors, they will have ample sharp objects to slice each other with."

Therapist: "Those sticks are simply decorative, and the vase holding them adds to a home-like atmosphere. The mirrors are there because I will use them to address body image issues. I really think you are stretching the potential behavior of women coming into a treatment environment."

Lieutenant: "I think you are stretching your trust in the inmates coming into this correctional facility. Has the superintendent seen your office?"

Therapist: "He's the one who told me to decorate my office as I would choose. Make it feel like home, is what he said. If you have a problem with my office, you should take it up with the superintendent!"

Lieutenant: "Uh huh.... okay then. I still feel the need to inform you that this office is a crime scene waiting to happen. If things get out of hand for you, use your radio and call my officers for help."

Therapist: "Thanks! However, I don't believe I'll need to. Speaking of radios, have you seen mine? That thing is so big, I always end up setting it down and then I walk off without it"

Lieutenant: "I've gotta go. I hope you find your radio. You're going to need it."

Sharing

The residents at the facility were allowed to purchase items from the canteen. There was a list of commissary items to choose from, such as snack foods, candy, soda, basic hygiene items and make-up.

Canteen items always presented a concern for the security officers as it was sometimes challenging to manage behavior when it involved these items. The lieutenant wanted to make it clear that the residents and their canteen items would be managed by officers.

Lieutenant: "I draw the line when it comes to inmates sharing canteen items, or any item for that matter. It's nearly impossible to manage from a security standpoint. No sharing of canteen items will be allowed. If any inmate is caught sharing, my officers will issue them a class three disciplinary incident report. The consequence for sharing will be a restriction of the inmate's privilege to order canteen items the next week."

Therapist: "Are you serious? You want to give a class three disciplinary write-up for something I would want to give them a certificate for?"

Lieutenant: "Okay, I really need you to hear me on this. Sharing is not what you might think it is in a correctional facility. I have witnessed where acts of sharing resulted in bullying, and even violence. From a security perspective, sharing is a major issue on the unit."

Therapist: "From a treatment perspective, sharing is encouraged. It shows empathy, compassion, building relationships, and connectedness. I don't understand where you are coming from. How does sharing result in violence?"

Lieutenant: "I understand in a normal environment that 'sharing is caring,' but in a correctional environment, sharing is, 'now you owe me.' Sharing is all too often, in reality, an act of selling, as opposed to sharing. The cost for accepting a mere candy bar can lead to bullying, violence towards another inmate, or even sexual favors. I'll give you one example. I witnessed a docile but large offender walk across the dayroom and start beating on another offender who was sitting at the table. There had been no prior interaction between the two of them. The fight seemed to come out of nowhere. After we broke the fight up, I asked the offender why he assaulted the other offender. He said, "I had to, because that was the cost of the bottle of shampoo I got." You see, the offender who sold the shampoo was the one who wanted the other offender beat up. So, there it is. Therefore, I need to advocate against sharing. It is an example of the worst-case scenario. Fact is, in some facilities, inmates can get killed over canteen items."

Therapist: "I have a hard time accepting that these women will receive a violation for something like sharing a candy bar with her cellmates. The women coming here are adults. There is a big difference between women and men. I'm asking you to please understand the gender-specific differences between the two and forego sanctioning a woman who has empathy for her peer."

Lieutenant: "I disagree. It has nothing to do with gender. It has everything to do with an oppressed population sharing in a secure environment. Canteen items become items of high value. They are like currency for people in secure facilities. I'm telling you, if we don't manage this, we will see conflict amongst the inmates, and even fights over something as trivial as a bag of chips."

Therapist: "I disagree. I don't believe the women would 'throw down' and get violent over a bag of chips. Furthermore, I believe females are different than males in many ways. Women are, by nature, generationally primary caregivers. Caregivers start that basic process through feeding others. Really, go ask many different women how they show someone that they love them. I'll bet you anything the majority will say, 'by cooking for or feeding them.'"

Lieutenant: "I'm not going to entertain a debate with you that a female population can manage sharing in a secure environment better than males. I don't believe it has anything to do with gender. There will be no sharing on the housing unit and that's my final stance. If you want to let them share their canteen items in your trauma group, then go ahead. But you should make sure the person sharing has enough to share with everyone in the group. Or, I guarantee you will have problems.

I can see letting the inmates share with all the other inmates in a structured environment, such as one of your trauma groups. But letting inmates share in the housing unit with a select few in front of other inmates is just mean and will result in conflict."

Therapist: "I understand that. However, I don't think you'll be able to monitor what sharing might occur in rooms between one roommate and another anyway. I would much rather have a rule that dictates 'no bullying will be tolerated,' rather than a 'no sharing will be tolerated' rule. It is about the words used to describe an event. I just can't agree with a rule that is mandating 'no sharing is allowed.'"

Lieutenant: "I know sharing takes place between roommates and I know my officers could never prevent that. My officers and I don't care if roommates share. Roommates will often manage the sharing without difficulties, and if a problem does occur between roommates, I'll split the roommates up. I am referring to sharing which takes place out in front of the other inmates. I am trying to protect the inmates who are weaker or considered outcasts. What happens in the dayroom can and will be managed by my officers. They will keep inmates from bullying or excluding a weaker or less-liked inmate.

Therapist: "Then why not make a rule that states, 'no bullying,' rather than 'no sharing'?"

Lieutenant: "We do have the expectation that inmates are not to bully other inmates. You're not understanding what I am trying to prevent. I'm not trying to prevent the honest and equal act of sharing. I'm trying to prevent conflict that results from sharing between an oppressed population in a secure environment. In most prisons and/or jails, very little is done to manage the sharing or selling of canteen items. As a result, inmates begin to manage it themselves. If you ask people who have spent time in jail or prison, I believe most will tell you the strongest and often meanest inmate has used canteen items as a way of exerting dominance over the rest of the population. I don't want to see this on my housing unit. This is what I want to prevent. You're asking me to manage bullying. This is extremely difficult to manage with an oppressed population in a secure environment. Bullying is very difficult to prove unless it is directly witnessed by an officer. A bullied person is bullied because they are often easily intimidated. When an inmate tells me someone is being bullied, and I then question the bullied inmate, that inmate usually won't admit being bullied because of the fear of the repercussions from the bully."

Therapist: "Let's just agree to disagree."

Lieutenant: "You can say that again…"

Training

The therapist was always confused as to how the staff were such good people, but so stuck in the fear of the possibilities the residents would hurt each other, or someone else. The lieutenant must have explained to her a thousand times that the training provided to the staff prepared them for this possibility. But it wasn't until she attended a training session where she saw it for herself. This training was mandated for the officers and they were required to attend numerous times before. It was the inmate manipulation training.

The training was primarily a video of several examples as to how inmates can, and will, manipulate their way into everything, from getting staff to give them a soda, bring in drugs, have sex with them, divorce their spouse and destroy a career. The video went into great detail, explaining and warning officers how an inmate will simply ask how your day was going, then from there, the inmate has successfully manipulated the officer. Nothing was left out.

The training video presented an openly arrogant inmate, and he speaks personally as to how he victimizes correctional officers. It presented the inmate as a powerful manipulator who can fool even the highest quality staff.

> ***Therapist:*** "Why are we watching this garbage?"
>
> ***Lieutenant:*** "This is a departmental mandated training for all correctional staff. That's why you are here as well. This is what I have been trying to tell you. We are trained to look for this type of inmate behavior. You seemed a bit uncomfortable. What did you think?"
>
> ***Therapist:*** "What did I think? Seriously? Is this a joke?"
>
> ***Lieutenant:*** "No joke. This is real. Inmates do manipulate to this degree. You heard it straight from the inmate in the video."
>
> ***Therapist:*** "That training video is designed to put the fear of God in every staff person who watches it! It will create a wedge the size of the Grand Canyon between staff and our residents. I'm already worried about how the officers are going to treat the women here. We can't have this type of junk filtering into the

minds of staff who are expected to deliver treatment. It's junk and it's dangerous. I want it gone."

Lieutenant: "I don't think it's junk. Inmates can and have manipulated staff. This is appropriate training for the correctional environment."

Therapist: "That junk tells every staff person not to look a person in the eye, not to answer questions, and not to respond if asked how their day is going. It's in absolute opposition to the very basic attitude needed to deliver treatment."

Lieutenant: "I agree this kind of training is not conducive to the treatment culture and the relationship-based rapport you want between officers and inmates. However, it is appropriate for the correctional environment. This training teaches us to keep our distance from inmates and to keep interactions to a minimum. The treatment model, on the other hand, expects us to trust the inmates and to have open communication with them. This is so frustrating. As a manager, it is especially frustrating. Officers look at me and ask, "How can I follow the training and the expectations of the treatment requirements of the relationship-based rapport?" If they get manipulated by an inmate, the department's response is, 'we train you to keep your distance, it's your fault.' Yet, when officers keep their distance, and it then negatively influences the treatment environment, they are told, 'you need to open up communication.'"

Therapist: "I can only imagine how frustrating it must be. However, this training is not conducive to treatment. It's dangerous. The one good thing this video gave me was a clear understanding of why officers are so guarded, and how much more guarded they will be with the women if we don't fix this.

Can we at least explain to staff it only applies to a prison and to forget about it here?"

Lieutenant: "I have no control over what trainings the department mandates. In a militarized organization, upper management rarely, if ever, asks lower management for their opinions. They give orders. No one has ever asked me whether the training is applicable to the facility or the program agenda. The department gives the order and we all must attend. Even the therapist, and that's why you're here. If I was given the opportunity to provide input, I would say this training is not suitable for the treatment program. I do my best to support both positions when officers are rightfully frustrated by these two very opposing directives. It's not easy. Their point is undeniable, and I agree with them. I wish the department would create a different training for correctional officers working in a treatment environment."

Therapist: "I hope we can find our way around this."

CHAPTER TWO

Developing the Treatment Program
Planning Meetings Become the Boxing Ring

The superintendent's office became the battleground for the planning meetings. For weeks, they discussed why they "must" or "must not" implement a policy. They were professional, yet unbarred. The meetings were sometimes loud, often frustrating, full of detail, and largely disputed. DOC policy references were often thrown at the therapist and she would hit back with treatment research findings. Security would present questions such as, "Do you know what a street drug would do on the unit?" She would kick back answers such as, "if you do even one strip search, I will walk." Her treatment ethics would simply not allow her to take part in a treatment facility that conducted strip searches.

The meetings got right down in the mud. They were dirty, loud, bizarre, and sometimes aggressive. They were also fun, full of laughter, bonding and progressive. They never did reach full agreement on some topics, but somehow, after months of discussion, they would often land on, "okay, the policy won't be removed, but we will not implement it unless absolutely necessary."

They became a team. They grew to respect their different perspectives and gained a common understanding that a safe and successful program was the goal. Despite some uncertainty on all parts, there was also a growing sense of relief.

The Application and Screening Process

The Riverside Recovery and Reentry Program was designed to treat adult females incarcerated from the jails and or prison, who were near, or at the end of their sentences. After completion of the program, they would be released back into the community. This provided a very strong incentive for the residents at Riverside to comply with program rules and expectations. As a result, this ruled out offenders who had current long term or life sentences, and focused primarily on inmates whose crimes coincided with Montana's Top 10 Criminal Offenses List. The discussions and resulting decisions of how the residents would be accepted into the program involved many people.

> ***Therapist:*** "It's very important that the applications be completed by the women themselves. It's my understanding that some departmental personnel would complete the application which they feel is suitable for the potential resident. On the application, I would like the question, 'Why do you want to attend a trauma treatment program?' This will help me to determine whether an applicant is truly serious about working the program. I could find authenticity in their answer."
>
> ***Lieutenant:*** "I agree completely. I want the people we select to actually want treatment. A person must truly want the help in order to get the most out of treatment. I believe one of the reasons correctional systems have such high recidivism rates is because people are forced into treatment programs, and/or because the system gives an ultimatum, such as, go to prison or go to treatment. This is not a clear choice. People in this case are not always choosing treatment, instead they are doing the only thing they can to avoid prison."
>
> ***Therapist:*** "I agree, and that's exactly why I want that question on the application."

Lieutenant: "My understanding is some treatment professionals believe sending someone to treatment when they don't want treatment can be successful because, while in treatment, the person may realize they need and want treatment. While this certainly can be true for some, I think it is far less often the case than believed. In my experience, facilitating behavior groups in a correctional facility, I have quickly picked out the people who have no real interest in treatment because they are forced to attend. They're often disruptive to the group and/or mock the lesson, preventing not only themselves from benefitting from the treatment, but also preventing the other willing participants from receiving treatment. I believe this is one reason we see such high recidivism rates from treatment programs implemented by corrections. The primary benefits an inmate should get from treatment is the treatment itself. The correctional system needs to stop grabbing people by the ear and dragging them into treatment."

Therapist: "I agree with you. However, I would choose treatment over prison or more jail time, if I were in their position. That's something we will need to pay close attention to. I agree that if a person is here, but shows no real interest in treatment, they should be removed from the program. You're right, it can be disruptive for others. However, I don't know if it's possible to identify just those wanting treatment. But once they get here, their behavior might indicate their true desire."

Lieutenant: "I'm in favor of removing any inmate who disrupts or takes away from the integrity of the treatment we provide. If they don't want to invest a sincere effort into their treatment, they should be removed from the program. I take this stance because I care about upholding an environment which supports treatment for all people who are serious about working their program."

Therapist: "I agree with you."

Lieutenant: "I think this program is on the right track to finding the right inmates because we are at least asking the inmate to tell us why they want to work a trauma treatment program. That's a great place to start. How are you going to assure that people applying have trauma needing to be addressed?"

Therapist: "That won't be a problem. They're all are coming from a jail or a prison. Everyone who is incarcerated has trauma, if not before, then certainly after incarceration. Strip searches alone do that. In addition to trauma related to incarceration, there is ample research showing trauma related to people who engage in criminal behavior and have addictions.[6] Many addictions are a result of a person's past trauma. It's my belief that trauma itself is primary, and addiction is a secondary symptom of trauma. Many times, people self-medicate because of the past trauma. That being said, one way we can measure trauma is through the Adverse Childhood Experiences (ACE) assessment.[7] The applications will help the screening committee rule out those we don't think are appropriate for our program. Our nurse should be able to identify those people whose health issues may require a higher level of care. I will also provide input about applicants whose mental health needs may require a higher level of care."

---

6 Matheson, Flora I. (2012) *Implications of Trauma among Male and Female Offenders.* Ontario, Canada. https://www.mdpi.com/1660-4601/9/1/97

7 Starecheski, Laura. (2015) *Take the ACE Quiz – And Learn What It Does and Doesn't Mean.* https://www.npr.org/sections/health-shots/2015/03/02/387007941/take-the-ace-quiz-and-learn-what-it-does-and-doesnt-mean

Lieutenant: "I expect something will be in the screening process to rule out recent violent behavior as well."

Therapist: "I am sure the superintendent will see to that."

Managing Program Expectations

Completing the hourly requirements for each area of programing would be self-directed by the residents. Each resident was mandated to complete 'X' number of hours for each module of the program.

All aspects of the daily program schedule were defined in the Resident Handbook and were given to the women before they applied. Thus, they were aware that everything in the program would be tracked by the hour of attendance, as well as their level of effort. If they refused a module of the programming, they were not issued a disciplinary consequence. Instead, they were marked as refusing that piece of programming. All refusals to attend programming were tracked and totaled each week.

The residents had a sense of control as to if they wanted to attend. If a resident strictly adhered to her schedule, she would complete the program in 16 weeks. If a resident missed an activity (no matter what that activity was) it would delay her graduation because that module may not be offered again for days, or even a week later. Although the women had self-direction and empowerment over their program participation, the officers managed their attendance and conduct.

Lieutenant: "We are going to let the inmates refuse programming whenever they want? We need to issue disciplinary incident reports when inmates refuse programming."

Therapist: "Yes, residents can refuse, if they choose. We don't need to be dealing out a disciplinary incident report to residents who refuse programming. We need to allow them to experience a natural consequence, as opposed to an authority figure issuing a sanction. The natural consequence to refusing programming is already in place, it will postpone their leave date."

Lieutenant: "What happens when an inmate attends programming but is not making an acceptable effort to participate in the treatment? We need the officers to have a way of managing inmates' efforts."

Therapist: "Define an acceptable effort of participation. What exactly does that mean to you?"

Lieutenant: "It can mean a lot of things. If an inmate is refusing to do the written work in the treatment group. This is unacceptable and the inmate should not get credit for the group. If the inmate is verbally disruptive or misbehaving. They should not receive credit. We need the officers to maintain a standard of participation as it relates to the inmate's effort to work the treatment. I hope you aren't suggesting the inmates manage their own level of effort, or that the inmates will manage each other's effort. I know some treatment centers do this. I don't like that type of treatment model. I want inmates to focus on their own individual program and not on each other. When they start judging and managing each other, it may create a conflict."

Therapist: "You have an uncanny ability to identify what is not acceptable. I would agree with the examples you gave. I believe the officer's presence provides structure and lends to the psychological safety of residents. But if the authority is used in a threatening manner, it will diminish that sense of security. I agree that residents should focus on themselves and their own treatment. I don't like the 'hot seat' approach where residents criticize each other, nor do I like people judging other people."

Lieutenant: "In corrections, we set rules and consequences for breaking those rules. This teaches inmates to respect authority and follow rules. It teaches them to follow the law."

Therapist: "No, that teaches them to resent the officers and want to rebel against the rules."

Lieutenant: "Let's just agree to disagree for now."

Program Schedule

The program schedule was designed to set times for all activities. The lieutenant and the therapist were assigned the task of developing the program schedule for the facility. The therapist drafted her preferred schedule and gave it to the lieutenant for his review. He took a quick look at it. The schedule, upon waking, would start with a gratitude circle, followed by breakfast, then fitness class and trauma group, then lunch. After lunch, was chemical dependency group, then strength finders' group, then meditation, then free time before dinner. After dinner was practicing positive group, free time on the housing unit, then a gratitude circle once again. Meditation, one last time before lights out. The lieutenant immediately responded.

Gratitude Circle

Lieutenant: "What the hell is this? Gratitude circle, meditation, practicing positive? Are you serious? When do we all hold hands and sing kumbaya?"

Therapist: "I'm not sure I understand. What seems to be your problem now?"

Lieutenant: "Well, beginning with this gratitude circle. What is this? Do they all stand in a circle and be grateful for being locked up in jail or prison? Are they supposed to be grateful for being separated from their kids, or even losing custody of their kids? I'm not sure you realize what kind of people are coming here."

Therapist: "Yes, I have an idea of who will be attending our program. Women who have been incarcerated for a long time and who are seeking treatment. They will already feel a sense of gratitude based only on the fact that they are moving through the correctional system, which means they are one step closer to being with their families. There is evidence-based research on the benefits of feeling gratitude, including an increased psychological well-being and keeping suicidal thoughts and attempts at bay. Scientific studies prove that being grateful improves physical health. Grateful people are less likely to feel pain and more likely to take care of their health. Gratitude improves psychological health and reduces depression."[8][9][10][11][12][13] If our program can help them feel grateful, they'll experience a deeper healing. From your security perspective, I would think you would be pleased, because gratitude will reduce the possibility of violent behavior."

Lieutenant: "Okay, I understand the benefits of being grateful. You have this group scheduled for 30 minutes. How am I

---

8 Emmons, Robert, a researcher on gratitude, states "Gratitude reduces a multitude of toxic emotions. Gratitude enhances empathy and reduces aggression."

9 Applied Psychology: *Health and Wellbeing* (2011). https://iaap-journals.onlinelibrary.wiley.com

10 Journal of Applied Sport Psychology (2014). https://www.tandfonline.com

11 The Journal of Personality and Social Psychology (2017). https://psycnet.apa.org

12 Ziegler, Erin Holaday. *Gratitude as an Antidote to Aggression* (2011). University of Kentucky https://psychology.as.uky.edu/gratitude-antidote-aggression

13 Kleinman, E. M., Adams, L. M., Kashdan. T. B., & Riskind, J. H. (2013). Grateful Individuals Arc Not Suicidal. *Personality and Individual Differences*, 55(5), 595-599. https://www.sciencedirect.com/science/article/abs/pii/S019188691300192X

supposed to manage their participation in a group like this? What if they simply tell the group they are not grateful for anything? How do I make a person, who most likely has more reasons to feel ungrateful, say they are in fact grateful?"

Therapist: "You could have them state three things they currently are grateful for and have them expand on why they have gratitude for those things. You could also pick a subject and ask them to find something they are grateful for related to that subject. The sky is the limit. Be creative."

Lieutenant: "They don't train us to be creative. I'm trained to follow orders."

Therapist: "Well then, how about you follow this order. Get creative."

Lieutenant: "I don't take orders from you and you may think this is simple, but my officers and I need to know how to manage things like participation expectations. The group is scheduled for two 30-minute blocks of time each day. I need to understand this so that I can instruct my officers on how to have consistency when approving or denying program credits. I must think of the worst-case scenario in a resident's program participation. In this case, it's clear what would be appropriate participation, but where is the line between appropriate and unacceptable?"

Therapist: "As long as a resident participates for the length of time allotted, she should get credit. I really don't think you are going to have a problem with this. The women are not going to want to stay longer because they didn't participate in a gratitude circle."

Fitness Class and Recreation

Fitness class was scheduled to be held each week, Monday through Friday, and it would be conducted by the fitness instructor. The focus would be on weight training and yoga activities.

In addition, officers would manage recreational activities held in the evenings, as well as on weekends and holidays. Participation would be necessary in order to graduate from the program. It was necessary to have standards in place to manage the residents in their participation.

> ***Lieutenant:*** "During recreational activities, we will monitor for effort, good conduct and teamwork. Inmates will not be judged on their skill set. Most of my officers are willing and even interested in participating in the rec activity. This adds to our ability to manage behavior.
>
> The fitness instructor can focus on weight training and yoga, and the officers will facilitate recreational games, such as basketball and softball."
>
> ***Therapist:*** "There is plenty of research defining the psychological and physical benefits of exercise. Walden University published an article on how exercise can help alleviate anxiety and depression, decrease stress, increase self-esteem and self-confidence, boost memory and brainpower, and help a person achieve better sleep.[14] I am all for maintaining a physical fitness component to our program, but I do think we need to be careful about how we supervise the women, and not set them up to resist it."

---

14 Walden University (2013-2014). *5 Mental Benefits of Exercise*. https://www.waldenu.edu/online-bachelors-programs/bs-in-psychology/resource/five-mental-benefits-of-exercise

Lieutenant: "I agree. Not only is physical activity beneficial to the residents, but from a security perspective, daily recreational activity releases energy which, if not released through exercise, can end up being released through disruptive behavior on the unit."[15]

Therapist: "We know that some of the women have health issues. I think we should have the nurse define all levels of physical participation expectations based off her health evaluations for each woman. She is the expert and the only one who will have access to the medical charts."

Lieutenant: "I agree. We'll follow the nurse's directives when managing a resident's level of participation."

Meditation

Lieutenant: "I see you want the residents to meditate twice a day. I'm opposed to this for several reasons. First, I can tell you right now, they will never do it. How do I make them do this? Do I demand that they all sit on the floor with their legs crossed, arms outstretched, palms up, touching their thumbs to their fingers as they all hum in unison? This is ridiculous. You need to pick something different for them to do."

Therapist: "Meditation is one of the best practices a person can undertake. It's an essential part of this treatment. There is evidence-based research showing many benefits, emotionally, mentally, physically and spiritually.[16] It can help with addic-

15 https://outdoor-fit.com/mental-health-benefits-exercise-prison

16 https://eocinstitute.org/meditation/141-benefits-of-meditation/

tion by reducing cortisol, which is damaging. Meditation also improves memory, concentration and optimism. It can help with controlling anger and reducing anxiety and it helps with PTSD. Meditation can awaken intuition, deepen awareness and increase connectedness. I can't possibly list the plethora of benefits that have been proven through scientifically researched evidenced-based studies. It's a crucial part of the program and I won't pick something different. Meditation will be a part of this treatment program."

Lieutenant: "That's all very fascinating. However, again, you're not answering my question. How do we manage something like this? Is this even something we can implement in the program? We can't force them to participate in a spiritual activity."

Therapist: "We are not forcing anybody to participate in any activity. Each person will undergo a screening process, and part of that process is their willingness to complete hours of treatment necessities. They will know and must agree to the expectations and requirements before they are accepted into this program. As far as forcing a person into a spiritual practice, meditation is not necessarily considered spiritual, although it can be for some. In this program, it will be used to slow down brain activity to allow for a healing process that might not occur without it. The women can meditate while lying in bed."

Lieutenant: "I'm still struggling to understand how this is supposed to work. When my officers conduct a visual check on them, how do we know if they are meditating? If they are lying in bed with their eyes closed, they could be sleeping for all we know."

Therapist: "It's okay if they're sleeping. You need to let go of the idea that you can control them. You can only control a person up to the point that they allow it. If they are watching tv, or reading a book, or anything that clearly shows they're not relaxed and breathing calmly, then you'll know they are not meditating. That's how you can determine whether they'll get credit or not."

Lieutenant: "You want us to give them program credit for breathing and sleeping?"

Therapist: "Yes."

Lieutenant: "This is unbelievable…."

Strengths Finder

The therapist understood well that the women accepted into the program were almost certainly coming from relationships, environments and histories that focused on and reinforced their weaknesses. So, she insisted on two things: that all incoming residents take a StrengthsFinder© assessment, and that the weekly programming include "strength finders" groups.

StrengthsFinder 2.0 is a book authored by Tom Rath.[17] Mr. Rath, states:

> "We were tired of living in a world that revolved around fixing our weaknesses. Society's relentless focus on people's shortcomings had turned into a global obsession. What's more, we had discovered that people have several times more potential for growth when they invest energy in developing strengths instead of correcting their deficiencies."

The therapist believed it was critical to the women's healing and growth that they discover, or rediscover, their strengths and focus on those instead of their deficiencies. She also believed it was very important for all staff, including

17 Rath, Tom. (2007). *StrengthsFinder 2.0.* Gallup Press https://www.amazon.com/StrengthsFinder-2-0-Tom-Rath/dp/159562015X

the superintendent, to take the assessment. This would help accomplish two things: they would better understand how demoralizing it was for those who were incarcerated where all the focus was on their deficiencies; in addition, they would be better equipped to help the residents if they first learned more about themselves and their own strengths.

Therapist: "Have your officers completed the StrengthsFinder Assessment? And, if so, what did they think of it?"

Lieutenant: "I read it. It was an easy read and I agreed with its basic premises. And I completed my assessment. I assigned all the officers to read it and take the assessment as well, and when they complete it, they will send me a written report on what they think of the book and assessment. My first impression of the book is it's short and not much to it. There doesn't seem to be much material to cover. How are we going to run a group four days a week for four months from this little thing? After you've received and read the strengths that the assessment identifies, then what? How many times can someone possibly talk about the five strengths the assessment identifies?

Therapist: "In this group, your officers can be as creative as they want. They could really find value and meaning in their role on the housing unit. For example, they could create a scenario, and then ask residents to apply their identified strengths to resolve the scenario's problem. The sky is open on this, and if your officers are encouraged to be creative, they may really enjoy this part of the program. I can print off some subject topics to help them get started. For example, they might present a question to the group such as, 'how can you use your strengths to avoid criminal behavior?' Or 'how can you use your strengths to overcome your addiction?'"

Lieutenant: "Okay, get me those subject topics and we'll go from there."

Practicing Positive

The therapist's program schedule continued to baffle the lieutenant as each new module was introduced. Positive Psychology interventions are theoretically grounded and empirically validated instructions, activities, and recommendations designed to enhance well-being.[18]

Lieutenant: "What is 'practicing positive'? Is this when inmates all get in a group and pretend being locked up is a positive thing?"

Therapist: "Look, I get this is very different from anything you've done before. You are most likely right that the women won't be feeling positive about being incarcerated. That is precisely why this group is needed. There is ample evidence-based research showing positive psychology practices are beneficial and successful in changing behavior."

Lieutenant: "So, you want this group to be facilitated by officers on the housing unit. Please tell me, how do we get inmates to practice positivity in a correctional facility?"

Therapist: "I have all of the worksheets ready for your officers to help them facilitate the groups. They come from the Positive Psychology Institute which has developed a field of study on human flourishing.[19] It focuses on the positive aspects of life

---

18 https://positivepsychology.com/what-is-positive-psychology-definition/

19 Practicing Positive Worksheets (2009). https://www.google.com/search?q=practicing+positive+worksheets&rlz=1C1GCEA_enUS828US846&oq=practicing+positive+worksheets&aqs=chrome..69i57.10824j1j7&sourceid=chrome&ie=UTF-8

that make life worth living. The women will be applying this approach toward looking at life in a different way. This approach is designed to complement traditional psychology. Each worksheet will take roughly half an hour to an hour to complete. After completion, I suggest you have the residents share, if they choose, or your officers can lead the groups in an overall discussion. If any of your officers need assistance, I will help."

Lieutenant: "Okay, get us the worksheets and we'll go from there."

Specialized Treatment

The specialized treatment components of the program were to include trauma and chemical dependency treatment, as well as HiSET®[20] education, parenting classes and medical treatment. These would consist of group treatment as well as one-on-one sessions, specific to the individualized needs of each resident. All aspects of specialized treatment would be delivered in a trauma-informed manner. This was deemed to be a huge priority. The therapist explained the difference between 'trauma-informed' and 'trauma responsive' to the lieutenant.

Therapist: "'Trauma-informed care' is the priority of this program. It is a strengths-based framework that is grounded in an understanding of, and responsiveness to, the impact of trauma. It emphasizes physical, psychological, and emotional safety for both providers and survivors, and creates opportunities for survivors to rebuild a sense of control and empowerment.[21]

---

20 https://www.essentialed.com/students/hiset-academy?gclid=EAIaIQobChMI8b_G4d6E6gIVEB-tBh2uwghWEAAYASAAEgJHvvD_BwE

21 Trauma Informed Oregon. (2010) *What is Trauma Informed Care?* https://traumainformedoregon.org/wp-content/uploads/2016/01/What-is-Trauma-Informed-Care.pdf

While we are becoming trauma-informed, becoming 'trauma-responsive' is much more entailed. It requires all aspects of an organization to be involved. It includes programming as well as changing the environment to include language and values that reflect the qualities of being trauma informed. And it involves all staff to better serve clients who have experienced trauma.[22] The focus of specialized treatment is to have trauma informed care. The support from your officers for this approach is critical."

Lieutenant: "What does this mean exactly? Due to confidentiality reasons, officers are not allowed in the trauma groups. How can my officers support the specialized treatment when we know nothing about what is happening in these trauma and chemical dependency groups? As far as I am concerned, the officers are essentially expected to respond to any misbehaviors that may take place during the group."

Therapist: "Trauma-informed care requires all staff, including the janitor, receptionist, superintendent and everyone in between, to understand trauma and its impact on the residents. We want to create an environment where the residents will have a sense of control and empowerment."

Lieutenant: "You need to understand where you are. We are a correctional facility and the population we house are inmates. Many of them have a history of violence. The inmates can have a sense of control and empowerment over their own unique treatment but not over the facility or staff.

Therapist: "We are talking about the residents feeling in control of their life and empowered in their decision making. And for

---

22 Covington, PhD, Stephanie S. (2018) *Moving from Trauma-Informed to Trauma-Responsive*. Hazelden Publishing. https://www.hazelden.org/store/item/520203?Moving-from-Trauma-Informed-to-Trauma-Responsive

the record, this is a treatment facility, first and foremost, not a correctional facility."

Lieutenant: "I don't know who writes your paycheck, but mine is signed by the Department of Corrections! How are we supposed to be trauma "informed" when we don't know any details of what takes place in the specialized groups?"

Therapist: "Trauma-informed implies that the entire facility is on board all the time, not just for a two-hour group twice a week. This means the unit where the residents will live requires a trauma informed approach by you and your officers."

Lieutenant: "Again, you are not answering my question. My officers and I will follow directives. If being trauma-informed is what the order is, we will anxiously await information on the trauma the inmates are working through. We can then be trauma informed and responsive."

Therapist: "Not quite, trauma responsive care requires the entire organization and it's language, policies, and procedures be revamped to support being trauma responsive. We need to focus on being trauma informed first."

Lieutenant: "I think you underestimate how much you are really asking for when you suggest the whole organization comply with all this. I don't foresee the DOC revamping its policies and procedures to become trauma responsive."

Therapist: "I'm not focusing on the whole department at this point. The trauma group and the chemical dependency group will be facilitated by me and the chemical dependency counselor. We have spent a significant amount of time choosing the workbooks we are going to use, which have been peer-reviewed and researched. The groups will be held in the administration building. The women will attend twice a week. I hope this doesn't interfere with the housing unit schedule, as half the women will remain on the unit during group times."

Face-to-Face

The therapist approached the lieutenant one day in his office. By this time, he was fully aware of her stance against unclothed searches, her support of residents' sharing, and her treatment regimen. This was a face-to-face interaction that neither of them would likely forget.

This wasn't a planning meeting. What he ended up saying to her was not pre-planned at all. Although, by then, it had been brewing inside of him for quite some time.

Therapist: "Mr. Johnson, I want to connect with you. Do you have a minute?"

Lieutenant: "Sure, come on in. I'm just finishing up something. Have a seat."

Therapist: "I feel like we all need to get on the same page. Your officers are an integral part of the treatment program. They will be the ones spending the most time with the women. It's important that they believe in this program."

Lieutenant: "Look, I'm going to be completely honest with you. I think what you're doing here is dangerous and I believe it will get someone hurt. Not conducting an unclothed search on the inmates will put people at risk. I think allowing the inmates to share is going to result in conflict on the unit. I have a responsibility to prevent people from being hurt or bullied. I don't think treatment like the gratitude circle and meditation is going to work with these inmates. I don't think you know the kind of people they are. I don't think it's going to work. But I'll tell you this, it won't fail because my officers or I do anything to cause it to fail. We will do this your way and we'll do it to a "T". I may not agree with your approach, but I'll see to it that it's done to the best of our abilities. I'll sell this trauma treatment to my officers because I have confidence in them. They are good at what they do. They will keep this place safe. No matter what the situation is, they will keep this place safe."

Therapist: "Well, what am I supposed to do with that? This program is going to fail, and it will be my fault? I am angry and relieved at the same time. This is a weird feeling. I wish you didn't think this program is going to fail. However, I am happy that you are committed to running the program to its fullest potential. I like the sense of integrity coming from you. I just wish you would take a course in communication."

Lieutenant: "Please understand, just because I disagree with you, and am willing to tell you, doesn't mean that I'm being mean. I understand most of what I have said must come as a shock to you, but this is my truth, and you have asked to "connect." So, like it or not, now you know where I am coming from."

Therapist: "This program will work."

CHAPTER THREE

Working to Blend
The Therapist Hands Out Rocks

The lieutenant walked into the security office one day. From this location, the officers were able to watch the events of the housing unit dayroom. He noticed that the therapist had all the residents gathered in the dayroom and one of the residents was reaching into a bag held by the therapist. He turned his attention to the officer on duty and asked:

Lieutenant: "What is she doing now?"

Officer: "She is conducting a rock ceremony."

Lieutenant: "What the hell is a rock ceremony?"

Officer: "She is letting the inmate who is graduating next week pick a rock from that bag. And then, I guess, she reads about the healing powers the rock has. I'm not really sure."

Lieutenant: "Rocks are contraband!"

Officer: "Yah, I know. But she's the therapist. What am I supposed to do?"

When the group ended, the lieutenant approached the therapist.

Lieutenant: "Ms. Champagne, may I speak with you for a minute?"

Therapist: "Sure, what's on your mind?"

Lieutenant: "So...... what were you doing out there? What's in the bag?

Therapist: "Crystals. I was having a 'well wishing' closure ceremony. It's important for the women to be able to say goodbye. The crystal is something they can take with them to remember all the good wishes the other women gave them. It's therapeutic. Why do you ask?"

Lieutenant: "Rocks are contraband. We don't allow inmates to have rocks on the housing unit. Sometimes they try to bring a rock in from the recreation yard and, when they do, we confiscate the rock and may even issue them a disciplinary write up for it. And now your handing them out?"

Therapist: "Why is a rock considered contraband? How could a small crystal be a security risk?"

Lieutenant: "Have you ever heard of a lock in a sock?"

Therapist: "A what...?"

Lieutenant: "A lock in a sock. It's when a padlock is dropped into an inmate's sock. The inmate can swing that lock in a sock, using it as a weapon. Replace the lock with a rock and you have the same weapon."

Therapist: "The women are not here to fight, they are here to receive treatment for trauma. I can somewhat understand your security thinking, but honestly, I do not believe we are going to have any issues like that."

Lieutenant: "I understand what you are trying to do. However, in the future, will you communicate with me ahead of time when you are implementing or planning to use something new, something we may consider to be contraband or a security risk?"

Therapist: "You think everything is contraband or a security risk. I'll do my best to communicate. However, I ask you to understand that I really have no idea of what you might consider contraband. I see the women as people first. I don't see them as a criminal."

Lieutenant: "I understand, for sure. That is why I ask you to keep me informed ahead of time. I'm asking you to have your rock ceremonies a day or two at most before the inmate is scheduled to graduate so we don't have too many rocks on the unit, and not for any longer than necessary."

Therapist: "That's easy enough. I can do that."

Camp Riverside

One day when the lieutenant walked onto the housing unit, a group of residents stampeded towards him, hollering with excitement.

Group of Residents: "Mr. Johnson! Mr. Johnson! Can we sleep out on the rec field and have a campfire and roast marshmallows? We could get chocolate and graham crackers and have S'mores!?"

Lieutenant: "Have you lost your mind?! No! This isn't camp riverside. No, I'm not buying S'mores. There's no way I'm letting you all sleep out on the rec field. And you sure as hell can't have a fire! Ever!"

The residents all froze as they all looked at the lieutenant as if he had just crushed their dreams.

Lieutenant: "Who the hell is filling your heads with this nonsense?"

At that exact moment, the therapist walked onto the housing unit.

Group of Residents: "Ms. Champagne told us to ask you!"

Therapist: "Ask what....?"

Group of Residents: "We asked him! We asked him if we could sleep outside like you said!"

The lieutenant stared at the therapist for a moment, then he turned away and walked into his office.

Lieutenant: "Rhonda! You're killing me!"

Manifesting

The residents kept asking the lieutenant to buy them pizza for dinner. He couldn't figure out why they would ask him to do this. He could never justify buying pizza for the inmates on the taxpayer's budget. He would flat out tell them they would never get pizza.

Over the next few days, the lieutenant listened to the residents brag that they were not fazed by his refusal to buy them pizza. The therapist had taught them how to manifest what they want. And whether he believed it or not, they told him he would buy pizzas for them soon.

A week later, one of the officers reported to the lieutenant that he had found mice droppings on all the meals that were just delivered from the prison. The meals showed clear signs that mice had ripped into the plastic covered trays, seemingly taking random bites of food as if it were a buffet. Three days' worth of food! Breakfast, lunch and dinner, and the next meal delivery wasn't due for another day.

The lieutenant quickly called the food factory at the state prison and reported the contaminated meals, and the need to reorder anything, and fast. The food factory informed him they would not be able to send a delivery until the next day. The lieutenant went to report the situation to the superintendent.

Superintendent: "Are all the meals contaminated?"

Lieutenant: "Yep. All of them. I have meal replacements arriving tomorrow but what do you want me to do about dinner tonight?"

Superintendent: "Well...just buy them pizza for tonight."

Lieutenant: "What! Pizza? Can I buy anything but pizza? How about sandwiches, hot dogs, or hamburgers, anything but pizza."

Superintendent: "What's your problem?"

Lieutenant: "Nothing. Nothing at all, I was just thinking pizza might not be the best idea."

Superintendent: "Just get them pizza."

Lieutenant: "Fine."

The lieutenant couldn't believe it! He knew he would never hear the end of this from the residents. When he walked on the unit with stacks of boxed community pizzas, the level of cheering and hollering coming from the residents was overwhelming. They were shouting that their manifestation had worked. He just dropped the boxes on the unit table and went straight to his office and shut the door. Well, the truth is, he took a piece of pizza with him. Some can argue the whole thing was just coincidence, but something was very peculiar about it. Something happened, that's for sure."

For the most part, recreational activities were voluntary as to the degree of participation the residents were expected to have in the activity. Staff would encourage, organize, and even participate in the recreational activities, but they didn't force people to participate. Some residents were older, and some had medical issues restricting them from participating in certain activities. The nurse evaluated each resident's physical health and set the level of physical expectation for each resident. Residents with recreational restrictions were still required to join the group and were still expected to get some level of large muscle exercise during this time. This earned them the credits for the rec portion of the program required for graduation from the program. Sometimes, that level of participation might only involve walking, and that was accepted.

Sometimes, residents would resist participating in the activity. During these times, the officers would remind them that refusing to participate was ultimately their choice, but it seemed a little silly not to obtain the required program credit because they refused to hit or throw a ball for an hour. Residents weren't required to be athletic or skilled in the activity. They were only expected to give an effort, display good teamwork, and encourage each other. When communicated like this, it was easy to get them to accept and participate. Many times, the officers watched residents at the beginning of a structured rec show irritation or resistance to the structure. But most often, by the end of the activity, they were laughing and having a great time. Exercise is so important in healing and transformation. Sometimes they just needed a little push (metaphorically), or motivation through encouragement, to get them started.

Lieutenant

One day, I announced that we would be having a structured rec activity outside, and the activity was softball. While the women went to their rooms to get ready to go outside, one of the officers told me that one of the women was refusing to go out with the group. The officer had already done what they could to motivate and encourage her, but she still refused. "Is she sick?" I asked. "No," said the officer, "I don't think so. She is just sitting on her bed. But she seems upset or stressed about something, and I think she may have been crying, by the look of her eyes."

It's difficult to pick false names to identify the people I speak of because I've worked with just about every female name there is. I'll name this woman, "Victorious".

I went to Victorious' room and found her sitting on her top bunk with somewhat of a death grip on her pillow. I could tell that she had been twisting it up as if she were wringing out a wet towel. It was common for an inmate to refuse recreation or other parts of the program simply because they didn't feel like making an effort. Part of my job is to manage this, and when necessary, apply some pressure for residents to attend programming. Unfortunately, I wasn't as sympathetic as I should have been.

"What's going on?" I asked. She replied, "Mr. Johnson, I don't want to play softball." "Why not?" I asked. She dropped her head and shoulders in a passive manner, but tightened her grip on the pillow and said, "I just don't like softball." I should have caught on to the signs, but I assumed she was just having a lazy moment. I replied, "That's not a legitimate reason not to come outside with us. It's just a game of softball. Come on, get up, let's go. The fresh air will do you some good." She started pleading with me, "Mr. Johnson, please just let me stay inside. I don't feel well. I'll just go on sick bay. I know I'll have to stay in my room for the rest of the day and that's okay. I'll do it." "No," I said. "I know you're not sick. Now get up. You're coming outside with us and we'll talk about the level of participation you are expected to have once we get out there."

On reflection, I feel bad for my sternness towards her. I just didn't see it despite all the signs she was giving me. I was caught up in the control factor of preventing someone from having a lack effort in their program. It was probably only because of her soul's strength, and/or perhaps (I'd like to believe) my past efforts to support a positive rapport with her, that she didn't totally stop all communication with me. Or, even worse, act out physically against me in response to my lack of empathy.

By the time we were ten steps out of the building, Victorious was experiencing an extreme panic attack. She was crying hysterically. Her hands were shaking like electricity was being jolted through them. I was convinced, by this time, that there was clearly much more going on with her than simply not wanting to play softball. I did the only thing I could do. I radioed the therapist and told her that I needed her to come to the rec field right away. I think she could hear the urgency in my voice over the radio. Or, it's very possible she tapped into her intuitive sense because she seemed to respond in seconds. I made eye contact with the therapist as I pointed to the mess I had created with Victorious. The therapist didn't even bother waiting for a briefing from me, she just routed herself straight to Victorious and they began walking the commonly used walkway, which was just off to the side of the larger rec field where the rest of the women would play softball.

I noticed some of the other residents giving me their evil eye. It was obvious to me, they knew what I clearly didn't, and I couldn't help but get the message that they felt like I should have known what they knew. Still not knowing the details behind Victorious' issue with softball, I reorganized the other women to take the focus off the therapist and Victorious as they walked just a short distance away. The other women were able to refocus, but I believe it was only because they all had confidence in the therapist. I'm sure they were relieved knowing Victorious was in safe hands.

I often pitched to the women when we played softball. In the pitcher's position, I was able to watch the therapist and Victorious walking. Their circle route was approximately 40 yards directly behind the batter. While I pitched, I attempted to dodge every woman who was seemingly intently trying to hit line drives at my head. I was able (privileged) to watch the therapist address the exposed trauma that had been triggered within Victorious.

I couldn't hear what they were saying. I could only watch as they walked laps around the walking area. At first, the therapist didn't seem to be doing much of the talking, Victorious was doing most of the talking. However, I wouldn't describe it as talking because I could see her crying and her arms flailing around as she spoke with frustration and anxiety in her voice. After they walked a couple of laps, Victorious' arms were moving less erratically and I could see that the crying had passed. I then watched the therapist collect one of the baseball bats from the rec cart. This concerned me at first. I remember thinking, "Oh no, don't give a bat to a resident who is upset." My attention was heightened at this time. I even motioned to one of my officers to keep a close watch on them in case Victorious decided to attack someone with the bat.

They walked for a while and the therapist held the bat. Then I saw her give it to Victorious. My heart skipped a beat. It quickly became clear to me that Victorious did not want the bat. She was holding the bat with only two fingers and she held it far away from her body as she continued to walk. A couple of laps later, and I suppose possibly because the bat became too heavy, she moved the bat closer to her body, but still only held the bat with her two fingers. A few more laps later, she had a full grip on the bat. None of this happened quickly, mind you. The therapist spent over an hour out there walking in circles and talking to Victorious. Soon, Victorious was holding the bat with a full grip, and periodically, lightly swinging it around as they continued walking.

By this time, it didn't take a genius to figure out the bat could be a major factor in this issue, but I still had no idea what it was all about. As we were about to end rec and head back into the housing unit, the therapist announced that Victorious wanted to have a turn as the batter. All the other women applauded her. I was still wondering what the big deal was, after all, it's just a game of softball. So, with red, swollen, and teary eyes, Victorious stepped up to the plate. I told myself I had better make the perfect pitches to her. I felt I owed her, at least, that for my insensitive response to whatever the heck was going on. With one pitch, Victorious hit the ball hard and far. The residents exploded with applause and cheers. They cheered and screamed like people would if their own kid had hit the game winning homerun. The energy was explosive in support of Victorious hitting the ball. I was happy everyone else was so happy, but I still couldn't help being a bit confused as to why it was such a big deal. I admit, it was a great hit, no question about that. But why was everyone responding so strongly to it?

After Victorious hit the grandiose homerun, all the residents, including Victorious, were sent back to the housing unit. After all the residents were in their rooms, the therapist entered the staff office.

Lieutenant: "What the hell just happened out there?"

Therapist: "I'm not at liberty to discuss that. I will see if Victorious is willing to provide that information to you."

Lieutenant: "Wait a minute? You're not at liberty to tell me what just happened to Victorious? Why was she having a panic attack? Why was every other resident out there so obviously angry with me?"

Therapist: "You are asking me questions that I cannot answer at this time."

Lieutenant: "It seems as if my officers and I are the only people out there who have no idea what is going on. You gave an obviously angry and upset resident a baseball bat! Do you have any idea how concerning that was for me?"

Therapist: "I agree, you need to know, you would have great understanding if you could know. I just can't share that information with you at this time."

Lieutenant: "I need to know what's going on with these residents when their behavior becomes a security risk. I need to know why you gave a baseball bat to an emotional and arguably angry resident?"

Therapist: "The resident did not use the bat inappropriately. When are you going to trust that I may know something about what I am doing?"

Lieutenant: "Trust you? I did trust you. If I didn't, I would have shut down the game the minute you gave her that bat. Then, I would have walked over to you and ended whatever you were doing. Simply because I have to uphold a safe and secure environment. It is my job to ensure the safety and security of everyone in this facility, and that includes you. Trust is earned. It is earned by having the necessary transparency between security staff and treatment staff. If she would have hurt you or someone else, I would be the one who would have to answer for that. Not you. If you are going to take risks like this, I need to know why so I can make appropriate decisions pertaining to the security needs of this facility. I feel like it is you who does not trust me!"

Therapist: "Necessary transparency is not just between the security staff and the treatment staff. Necessary transparency is required by the resident and expected between a resident and a therapist. In the correctional system, residents have little trust, if any. I appreciate that you did trust me and Victorious. Thank you for that. I recognize that others in your position, with your level of responsibility, would have probably reacted differently."

Lieutenant: "When does this necessary transparency between officers and residents take place? Before or after a traumatic episode? I believe it is more helpful if officers working here have pertinent information before a traumatic episode so we can respond in a trauma informed and responsive matter."

Therapist: "In a perfect world, details would come out during the triggering event, or prior to the event. Most, if not all, of the residents believe the correctional system we work in has not been trustworthy. I understand your frustration. Please know that we are a work in progress and that there are still many things needing improvement. You should have the information, but I am not the person to tell you. That would be a breach of confidentiality. I will try to get permission from Victorious, or preferably have her explain things to you herself, so you may understand."

Lieutenant: "I need to know these things if you expect me or my officers to be trauma informed and responsive. I am trying to understand. I understand confidentiality and its very important role. However, why couldn't you or Victorious simply tell us she has some kind of trauma related to the game of softball? If I had known just that, I would not have pushed her to participate in the game. I would have excused her."

Therapist: "No person experiencing a trauma trigger knows what is going to trigger them at any given time. It's the nature of trauma and how it effects the body. If I could predict every trauma trigger out there, I would have informed you. But that is nearly impossible. I understand why you are so frustrated. I am expecting you to be trauma informed and responsive, while at the same time, I do not inform you of the nature of a trauma. It is counterproductive. I am sorry. Can we find a middle ground?"

Lieutenant: "Yes, I believe there is middle ground. Give us the necessary information so we can be trauma informed and responsive."

This event really impacted the lieutenant. A few days later, the therapist received permission from Victorious to inform him of what was behind all this. With Victorious' permission, and at her request, the therapist informed him that Victorious had been sexually assaulted and raped with a baseball bat.

The residents were aware of this because Victorious had shared about it in a confidential trauma group. The lieutenant felt he should have been more in tune with the non-verbal signs Victorious was giving when she told him she didn't like softball. He acknowledged his fault in this, but it would have been helpful if Victorious would have verbally informed him of the trauma. He, then, would have excused Victorious from the activity, with no consequence.

It is not Victorious' fault for not communicating with him. Not by any means. He was responsible for being aware of possible trauma in these women's lives and being attuned to such sensitivities. In other words, trauma-informed and responsive.

In a trauma treatment environment, or any treatment environment for that matter, it is essential that the residents trust the staff. If he had a little more trust established with Victorious, she may have felt safer in informing him of her trauma. With the therapist's help, he processed with Victorious in a counseling setting and apologized for any harm he had caused her.

Trauma-Responsive Victory

Therapist

Trauma triggers are often unpredictable. The example of Victorious' trigger(s) may seem obvious to the reader, but in most cases, being triggered is much more subtle than that. Oftentimes, it is a smell, a certain color, or a sound that triggers a person. Most people who get triggered have no idea what triggered them. Usually, they are doing something mundane, like shopping for groceries, when all of a sudden, they feel their heartbeat start to race, they feel like they can't breathe, and they find themselves in an all-out panic state, having no idea what went wrong between grabbing the milk and the eggs. And then, all of a sudden, they never want to go shopping again.

The brain processes a trigger as if the traumatic event is happening again, right in that moment. The body responds in the same way too. Victorious was tuned into her brain's warning of danger. She felt as if her rape was occurring again. She *knew* it wasn't happening, but she couldn't shake the *feeling* that it was happening again until she first recognized that she was safe.

When the lieutenant was first talking with Victorious, her brain wasn't able to comprehend much as her pre-frontal cortex was being flooded with cortisol, fogging up her ability to assimilate information.[23] Her brain was operating in the area that processes fear. The lieutenant and the unit staff did exactly the best thing they could to help her. They called in a therapist and allowed the therapist to take over, without swarming her. They recognized that something was off with her reaction, but they didn't insist on fixing it. On some level, the lieutenant and the unit staff recognized the signs and symptoms of trauma.

Victorious is brave. She regained her power that day and allowed her brain to understand that softball was a game she could continue to enjoy.

"The day I played softball, I was no longer a victim, I was Victorious."
Resident Testimony

Taking a Chance with a Facility Dog

The Chemical Dependency (C.D.) Counselor was most determined to obtain the superintendent's approval to get a facility dog. It took more than a few planning meetings before she was able to get the superintendent to stop wincing and chewing on the inside of his cheek to give her the green light to obtain a dog.

23 Bernstein, Rebecca. (2016) *The Mind and Mental Health: How Stress Affects the Brain.* Touro University Worldwide. www.tuw.edu/health/how-stress-affects-the-brain./

The lieutenant had his concerns about bringing a dog into the facility. This was due to his DOC training that taught him to be cautious of everything, along with the need to have complete control of anything and everything. His brain went straight to all the "what if's" pertaining to having a dog living at the facility. He quickly started creating worse-case scenarios. This line of communication always starts with, "What if?" and is closely followed by, "How do I control it?" He presented his concerns in the planning meeting the best that he could.

Lieutenant

"What if the dog bites someone? What if it knocks someone down? What if it gets in the way or bites a staff when we are involved in a use-of-force wrestling match with a resident? What if someone is allergic to dogs? What if a resident hurts the dog? What if sharing the attention of the dog becomes a problem? What if it poops on the floor!? What if... what if.... what if...???" Lastly, I stated, "There is no way I can control this."

It felt weird, not only arguing against a dog because I love dogs and have two of my own. It felt weird because in my heart, I loved the idea of having a facility dog. But my need to control everything overruled my true feelings on the matter. I just kept thinking, "It can't be done with guaranteed safety!" To avoid the risk, I advocated against getting a dog.

I lost the argument. The superintendent told me, "You and the C.D. counselor go pick out a dog and pick a good one." I thought, "Great!" Now if it turns out to be the disaster I have been debating as such, everyone can blame me for picking out the 'bad dog'.

Reluctantly, I left with the C.D. counselor to go seek out a dog for the facility. Our mission was to go to the Animal Shelter and interview dogs, in a dog prison, to find a dog, to fill the job of a so called 'therapy dog in a correctional facility'. During the trip, I couldn't help but think of the irony in all of that. Poor dog is going to go from one prison cage right into a correctional facility.

I had it in my head we had to get a female dog. I'm not sure why. I guess I figured a female dog would click better with the women in the facility. I knew I wanted a mid-sized dog that would be able to chase a ball or a frisbee. Other than that, I was open to knowing the right dog when I saw it.

When we arrived at the shelter, we informed the kennel employee of what we were looking for, and we then started our dog interviews. The kennel employee brought dogs in to meet us, one by one. All of them were of mixed breed. Abandoned, unwanted dogs left to the mercy of the selection process. Some dogs were too hyper, some were too small, some were way too big, and others just didn't have enough spark. Then, the employee brought in a black colored male dog with a white chest, his breed appeared to be mostly Border Collie. The dog went right up to the C.D. counselor, not too fast, and not to shy. He sat down next to her and laid his head in her lap. The dog then turned and looked at me, and I saw it immediately. It was in his eyes, and it was unmistakable. Gentle, loyal, aware, careful, and grateful. The C.D. counselor looked at me and let out a sound, "aww....". I replied, "Yep, he is the one." We spent a few more minutes with him, but the decision had been made, with zero doubt. I told the kennel employee, "We will take him."

On the way home, we knew we needed to pick a name before we got back to the facility or we would have to endure a months' worth of planning meetings before we would all agree on a proper name for him. We contemplated several different names before we agreed on "Chance". It supported the second chance we were giving him and the second chance we wanted the women to feel they had. Chance was now employed as the therapy dog for the facility, although he didn't have a lick of credentials or experience. He was, in fact, recently released from prison. But it was abundantly clear that he had the right personality for the job.

When we got back to the facility, it took a couple of days for Chance to settle in, much like it did for the women to adjust when they first arrive.

Lieutenant: "Now that we have a dog, we need to make some rules on managing him with the residents."

Therapist: "Rules? Why?"

Lieutenant: "We need rules. For example, no feeding the dog people food. Every resident and staff will want to feed him people food. I guarantee it. Residents will be slipping him food every chance they get, just so that he will like them. Do you want the dog to get overweight or be unhealthy?"

Therapist: "Yes! Of course! I want the dog to be overweight and unhealthy! Who do you think I am? Who has a dog and doesn't feed it treats? The residents will need to feed him treats to teach him to do tricks. How do you do that without treats?"

Lieutenant: "Fine! I'll buy nonfat treats and the officers can give them to the residents when they want to teach the dog tricks. No people food."

Therapist: "Good idea, if you can find nonfat treats."

Lieutenant: "I want a rule that when we utilize a use-of-force or cell extraction, the dog must be secured in another building. I don't want to be tripping over him while we are restraining an inmate, I mean, resident."

Therapist: "We are not going to have a 'use-of-force' or a 'cell extraction event'. We are a treatment facility. We treat. That is what we do. And speaking of treats, don't you need to go find nonfat ones?"

Lieutenant: "What happens if he bites someone? What happens if the residents aren't sharing time with the dog appropriately? What if a resident is allergic to dogs? What then? Who gets stuck picking up dog poop? All the residents will want to give him a bath. How do you decide who gets to give him a bath? We need rules for managing and responding to these situations."

Therapist: "Lieutenant Johnson, sir, can you just breathe for a moment?"

Lieutenant: "The dog will not be allowed in the residents' rooms overnight. That is a rule!"

Therapist: "Fine."

Chancing It

The lieutenant was obviously stressed because, on some level, he knew he could not control all the 'what if's' rolling around in his head. Some of his concerns proved to be true. The residents did slip Chance morsels and treats. Most of the staff brought in special treats for Chance, everything from rawhide to deer bones and ham hocks. Chance was spoiled and overweight. Everybody fed Chance, just not in front of the lieutenant.

Despite the lieutenant's concerns, Chance turned out to be a great addition to the facility. He was one of the first wins that came out of the planning meetings. Chance knew his role and he was perfect at it. If someone arrived at the facility in handcuffs, she was golden and in need of his love and protection. He loved big and protected bigger. The poor delivery guys! Chance barked and growled at them every time they came by. However, they, too, learned to bring him treats in order to be given access to some parts of the facility. Chance would allow them entrance, but only if they didn't get too close to the women. Chance was all about the women. They belonged to him and he belonged to them.

Chance had his own problems with the law. He was a habitual offender. He was a perpetual thief. This endeared him to the therapist. Most days, she would hear the maintenance man screaming, "Chance! Get back here! Chance drop that! Chance! Chance! Chance!" She would look out her window and see Chance running playfully with a hammer or screwdriver, or some tool the maintenance man needed. She could almost read Chance's thoughts, "Catch me if you can!" He often stole the gloves right off of the women's hands. Chance would sneak up on them as they were walking from the unit to the gym, then suddenly he would pounce, take the glove off someone's hand, then tear off into the field begging them to chase him. Of course, they couldn't do that. So, she would often hear the women screaming just like the maintenance man.

When Chance was allowed in the gym with the women, it was like watching a dog on an ice rink. The smooth floor made it impossible for him to cut a corner or stop when he wanted. Instead, he would cascade across the floor, taking out the residents like a bowling ball shattering the pins.

One of his favorite pranks was to hide behind the electrical transformer box that paralleled the sidewalk. Chance knew the women's schedule better than they did. He knew that every morning, at 9:00 a.m., the women would be walking in a line heading to fitness class in the gym. He would let a few women pass before he would shoot out from behind the transformer, pouncing on the unsuspecting one who didn't realize that he was there. Often, he would take them to the ground and get as many licks in as possible before someone would pull him off. There wasn't much disciplinary action taken against him. They just figured he was a 'lifer' in this prison, one with his own rules.

"Chance has helped me so much; words cannot begin to explain."
Resident Testimony

CHAPTER FOUR

Cultures Blend
Officers Become Correctional Counselors

The program was fully staffed, and each bed was occupied. The team was engaged in the program and things appeared to be on track. It wasn't perfect by any means, yet everyone was working together. There were still some extreme differences of opinion on some things. But, when a decision was made, everyone accepted it. The lieutenant and therapist worked relentless hours supporting the counselors in muddling through the oppositional policies and procedures, policies that were new and other policies that had been in play for so long. The lieutenant fully understood the value and role his counselors played in creating a positive culture in which the residents would feel safe. The therapist spent exhaustive hours transferring her accumulated knowledge to the lieutenant. In addition, she facilitated specific trainings on trauma informed and responsive care. Both were committed to the vision of the program and would go the distance to see its implementation. The process did not occur overnight. It took months of pruning, supporting, encouraging, and defending the newly adopted style of treatment in a prison environment. The correctional officers were thorough in their demand for integrity and adherence to both treatment and correctional policies. Many times, it did not seem possible to combine these two contrasting worlds. Because the correctional officers held such veracity in themselves, the work they did, and their commitment to the Department of Corrections, it required many discussions and thorough explanations to successfully transform their role. It was ultimately this team that shaped Riverside into the success it was.

The lieutenant had kept his promise. He had achieved a genuine 'buy-in' from his officers. They had become "correctional counselors".

The lieutenant led his team and encouraged them to be open-minded, and positively role modeled to those he supervised. The team was crucial to the success of this program and had come so far from their initial thinking of the program as Camp Riverside. The degree of unity was surprising, especially because it happened in a correctional setting entrenched in policies and procedures seemingly aimed at stopping a treatment environment like this from ever occurring.

> ***Therapist:*** "Lieutenant, you really are not the hard-ass that you have portrayed yourself to be."
>
> ***Lieutenant:*** "Hey! Don't go blabbing that to people. I have a reputation to uphold."
>
> ***Therapist:*** "Too late. The women are already on to your softer side. One of them stated to me, "Mr. Johnson has a heart. I could tell when he participated in the gratitude circle this morning."
>
> ***Lieutenant:*** "Well, don't encourage them! If they start thinking I've gone soft, I'll have nothing but problems. They need to know I won't tolerate misbehavior and/or lack of effort."
>
> ***Therapist:*** "Your correctional counselors have managed to put aside their prior harsh training and are now building a person-centered therapeutic rapport with the women. I know because several of the women are talking about trust when referencing them. Many of the women here have had bad experiences with men, and it is so healing for them to witness male correctional counselors behaving respectfully towards them."

Lieutenant: "I agree. Despite the prison and jail officer trainings, they have embraced the correctional counselor role. This was no easy task and I am so proud of them. They have become correctional counselors without losing control of the environment. In fact, it has contributed to the safety and security of the facility. It has fostered compliance from the residents more out of respect than from power and control."

Therapist: "That makes perfect sense to me. Power and control are always met with resistance. It also reflects SAMHSA's "Collaboration and Mutuality Key" approach.[24] People are more likely to work together when they feel they are equals. Are the correctional counselors implementing self-determination, critical thinking, and independence?"

Lieutenant: "Yes they are. I'll start with self-determination. The correctional counselors and I are constantly encouraging self-determination. Every day, all day, we encourage this with the residents. I witnessed one of my correctional counselors running the mile with the residents and encouraging all of them to push beyond their comfort zone and beat their best time. I don't order them to run the mile. They do it for the residents.

Next, critical thinking. The correctional counselors facilitate the 'Practicing Positive' groups, teaching a variety of critical thinking scenarios. When conducting one-on-one counseling sessions, they are challenging residents to reevaluate their thinking patterns and offering positive coping skills when needed.

Thirdly, independence. The counselors frequently remind the residents that they have the choice to refuse programming.

---

24 Substance Abuse and Mental Health Services Administration (SAMHSA)© https://www.samhsa.gov

We don't force any of them to work the program. They decide to attend or not attend, although we do provide incentives to participate. In addition, in the 'Strengths Finders' group, the residents are developing their own independent solutions to challenging situations."

Therapist: "I recognize the efforts you and your correctional counselors have made and I greatly appreciate what you have all done with this program. You have maintained safety and security by building therapeutic, relationship-based rapport. I saw one of the correctional counselors sit on the floor in a non-threatening manner and obtain items from an extremely upset resident. I am very proud of your correctional counselors and their ability to approach confrontation in this way. Our program is good, it's working, and that would not have happened without you and your correctional counselors. I want to continue to improve the program. By the way, what was that incident all about?"

Lieutenant: "We had just received a new resident who had a violent history and she was refusing to turn in her cowboy boots during the intake process. She told the correctional counselors she would fight anyone who tried to take her boots. Now, our training teaches us to ask a few times and then, after that, call for additional staff to forcibly take those boots right off her feet. Instead, the correctional counselor followed a therapeutic approach and through conversation, he was able to get her to take her boots off and turn them in without using force. The correctional counselors have stretched the bounds in leveling the power. But you need to know I will never ask them to give up full control. There is a line, and when a resident adamantly decides to cross it, we will use force if necessary. I do appreciate your acknowledgment on how we have extended that line far beyond what we were taught through departmental training. I admit, I am surprised we haven't needed to use force thus far."

Therapist: "Lieutenant, our program is working. Thank you for your part in that."

Lieutenant: "I believe these women are getting stronger mentally, emotionally and physically. I appreciate all you've done to help us get to where we need to be. Why do you believe the program is working?"

Therapist: "It's not what I see, it's what I hear from the women. They love it and tell me all the time how grateful they are to be here. They love this environment and feel safe in it. Now, they can begin to love themselves. How do you know it?"

Lieutenant: "I know it because my correctional counselors are telling me they see it working."

"Thank you for changing my life and believing in me.I never knew treatment could feel this good."
Resident Testimony

The Program from a New Perspective

The lieutenant couldn't help but acknowledge that the residents were not proving to be the trouble that he had expected. His correctional counselors continued to point out success in the program and the effects on the residents. He could tell they were truly seeing the residents as people, as opposed to troublemakers.

The correctional counselors spent more time with the residents than any other staff member, and they observed the residents outside the structured programming. They saw and interacted with residents during free time, the weekends and holidays, etc. They observed the residents when the residents didn't know they were being watched. Their perspective as to how the program was running and how the residents were behaving far exceeded anyone else's expectations. The lieutenant trusted their knowledge. The shift supervisors told the lieutenant that the correctional counselors were engaging more in the program and with the residents. They could see the correctional counselors were successfully building the needed relationship-based rapport and as a result, the residents were building trust with them. It was the feedback from correctional counselors and the shift supervisors which convinced the lieutenant the program was, in fact, successful.

"I love all the correctional counselors. They treat us like a person."
Resident Testimony

Gratitude Circle Comes Full Circle

The Gratitude Circle helped to build the rapport between correctional counselors and residents. The counselors' participation enabled the residents to see and accept them as more than just authority figures. Nearly every day, a resident expressed gratitude for a correctional counselor's help at some level. The correctional counselors' participation enabled them to express their gratitude for residents. The scheduling of the gratitude circle twice a day allowed for both first shift and second shift counselors to strengthen the bond between correctional counselors and residents. The lieutenant was convinced it was this level of respect between both counselors and residents which supported a safe and secure environment.

> ***Lieutenant:*** "I believe the Gratitude Circle is the most valuable and influential housing unit programming we offer. I really can't say enough about how being truly grateful for what you have can really change a person's life. It was something easily overlooked without the structure of this group being offered twice

a day. Starting and ending the day with thoughts of gratitude and appreciation has proven to be invaluable."

Therapist: "I agree. Gratitude Circle provides transparency and builds trust and open relationships between the staff and residents. This is another example of how this program uses one of the six key principles of SAMHSA©'s trauma-informed approach."

"I'm so grateful for Gratitude Circle, it helped me feel closer to other women and especially the staff."
Resident Testimony

Strength is Found in Strengths Finder Group

The Strength Finders group developed into a favorite among the residents. Each resident maintained a logbook of their written assignments. By the end of their program, they would have approximately sixty-four different individualized, scenario-based solutions to challenging situations. Some residents had hundreds of pages referencing how they could use their strengths. Residents were encouraged to keep their logbooks and read them beyond their graduation from the program.

Therapist: "The residents really appreciate the Strength Finders group. Your counselors are really connecting with the residents. How did you achieve this level of buy-in from them?"

Lieutenant: "They are doing a great job. The short answer is, I have intelligent counselors and I let them do their job with as little interference from me as possible."

Therapist: "I agree, but there must be more to it than that. The residents really enjoy this group. Many said it was their favorite group. When I asked why, a common answer was because the "teachers" do such a great job bringing meaning to the group. What's the long answer?"

Lieutenant: "After we first introduced the book, the counselors completed their own assessments and emailed me their strengths. I replied to each one, associating their strengths to their work ethic. I practically had the book memorized by the time I finished with all sixteen counselors and their five strengths. Then, I shared with them, in detail, how I viewed their strengths in their work. I hoped this would validate the assessment and display how their strengths support the purpose of this treatment."

Therapist: "The counselors must have found that validation and are now passing it on to the residents. They tell me the counselors are picking good topics and even participating in the group using their strengths from their own assessments. It's a great display of collaboration, another one of SAMHSA© key guidelines."

Lieutenant: "I do my best not to be a micro-manager. I believe if I don't trust my counselors, then I am doing something wrong, not them. I encouraged the counselors to manage this group based on what they feel is applicable to the residents and the mood of the residents. The counselors know the energy of the residents better than most staff. They spend the most time with the residents. I wanted them to use this knowledge, and I believe allowing them this freedom to pick the direction of the group each day supported their commitment to the group."

Therapist: "That is unique for an organization like DOC. Most organizations that follow a military style of leadership will not allow the people they supervise the freedom to feel ownership of the work they do. In fact, most mandate exactly how they want it done and how they should think or not think about it."

Lieutenant: "Residents have also told me they liked the group because it puts them in control of the process and the implementation of the successful outcome. They often told me, in most treatment curriculum, the lesson is all about cramming someone else's theory down their throat. Telling them exactly what they should do or not do. The Strengths Finder group allowed them to decide how they would see themselves through the situation with a positive outcome. They were in control of their treatment and I think when they reflect on the logbook, it will be like reading letters written to themselves."

Therapist: "I know they love the group! What is most often expressed to me is that they feel in control when they attend that group. They are empowered. It builds trust in themselves."

"I am learning of strengths I never knew I had. I'm learning I do have strengths which will see me through my challenges."
Resident Testimony

Meditation Works

Managing the residents during meditation periods seemed impossible when first presented to the lieutenant. He had to let go of the idea that he needed to control the process and confirm meditation was, in fact, taking place. The correctional counselors too, had to learn how to let go of control and focus on providing a quiet undisturbed environment, as opposed to "policing" the act of meditation. During the thirty-minute meditation periods, the counselors conducted one visual check on each resident. If a resident was reading, writing or moving around excessively, they were denied credit for that meditation session.

Residents were clearly informed of the minimum expectation for the meditation period. They were expected to be relatively still, focus on their breathing, and if they fell asleep, that was accepted. The therapist provided the residents with techniques to meditate. This seemed simple, but proved challenging for some residents.

> ***Lieutenant:*** "I have to admit, I thought the meditation piece of the program was a complete joke. There are still some residents who don't like it, but most see the benefits of it. Some residents who didn't like it in the beginning of their program are now looking forward to the meditation time."
>
> ***Therapist:*** "I have heard some women explain their initial concerns, but what are the reasons they are giving you that they don't like it?"
>
> ***Lieutenant:*** "I recall one resident who told me that we couldn't make her meditate. She said this in a challenging manner, in front of all the other residents in the dayroom. I could tell the residents had been discussing the legalities of the meditation piece of the program. She was the one who took on the voice of more than a few of the residents' opinions at the time. She told me meditation was against her religion. The rest of the residents stopped all their conversations and activities in the dayroom and waited for my response."
>
> ***Therapist:*** "Meditation is not a religious practice here. It can be for some, but the purpose here is to allow the body and mind to calm. We have many different guided meditations, some have a religious tone, and some don't. Some are guided meditations of nature sounds or drumming. I was careful to have a variety

to choose from to support empowerment, voice and choice, another of SAMHSA© guidelines. What did you tell her?"

Lieutenant: "I told her that I had no intention of forcing a religion or spiritual belief on her or even making her meditate for that matter. I told her that I couldn't make her, even if I wanted to. She doubled down and told me that I can't make meditation a required credit for the program. She said she should be able to read a book or write a letter because she doesn't like to meditate."

Therapist: "Writing a letter is not meditating, neither is reading a book. What did you say?"

Lieutenant: "I reminded her, as all the residents intently listened to our conversation, that she was the one who had completed the application to participate in the program. She received a program agenda before she made her decision to complete the application and participate in the program, in its entirety. No one forced her and no one was forcing her to stay, for that matter. Then, I told them all that anyone of them could quit the program, for any reason. It was their choice. One of them said, "If we quit, we will most likely go back to jail." I agreed that would be the most common placement if they chose to quit, because most of them left jail to partake in the program."

Therapist: "That is my understanding."

Lieutenant: "Then, I asked them to think of the process of returning to jail. I said, "Imagine yourself quitting because you refuse to take part in the meditation piece of the program, and as a result, you return to community jail. The first question you'll be asked by other inmates will most likely be, "Why are you here?" From there, if you chose to tell the truth, you would have to explain that you quit the program because you refused the meditation piece of the program. You would have to further explain that meant you refused to be relatively still in your room for approximately 30 minutes while you focused on your breathing and ultimately fell asleep. Then, I let them just think about that for a while. All remained silent for a few long seconds."

Therapist: "That's a great response. I'll bet they were too busy thinking about the meaning of what you just said."

Lieutenant: "I think the reality set in as to how minimal the expectation is. I encouraged them not to overthink it. Just lie down and relax. After that, their defensive postures and facial expressions dropped, and I never heard another opposition from any of them."

Therapist: "That is a good response and a great example of the therapeutic rapport, leveling of power, and self-direction, working to support compliance as opposed to the power and control approach. It takes a bit more effort in communication to present, as opposed to, "Do it because I said so, and if you don't, you'll get a consequence." But long-term compliance is far more achievable."

Lieutenant: "Our society has formed a fast lifestyle. We often move quickly as we live our lives, moving through our work, family needs, childcare, housekeeping, home improvements, education, entertainment, relationship needs, and all the many other responsibilities we must meet. We sometimes struggle to make time to even eat. Driving through the fast food restaurant to save time in order to meet the next deadline, whatever that may be. Deadlines rule our schedule and rush the living process."

Therapist: "The responsibilities we have do get to be overwhelming."

Lieutenant: "It's difficult to manage all these responsibilities and stay ahead of things. The rushed lifestyle becomes habit-forming. Now, add an addiction to the process and a person's mind really speeds up. A person can quickly become flat-out uncomfortable being still, both in body and in mind. I believe the meditation treatment helps many residents counter these habits of rushing through their decision process and the daily activities of life. It also proved to support calming behaviors on the housing unit."

Therapist: "I agree, I know it has helped so many learn to value and appreciate the slowing down of time that meditation allows for."

"I finally remember who I am, and I like who I am."
Resident Testimony

Recreation Provides Connectiveness

Having the correctional counselors participate in recreational activities allowed for connectiveness between them and the residents. The lieutenant didn't force correctional counselors to participate, although most did.

Residents ran a mile once a week. This was a structured rec activity, so all residents were required to participate unless the nurse had excused them for medical reasons. Most residents dreaded the mile-long run when they first entered the program. It was not a requirement to run the mile. Most would walk it, but even those that walked began to push themselves the best they could. Some would power walk, others would walk one lap and run the next. Usually when residents neared their graduation, many would be running the whole mile. Others who were younger or more athletic would run from the beginning of their program and push themselves to beat their time each week. Even those that ran the mile had the freedom to walk it if they chose. It was having this choice that proved to result in most residents giving their best effort.

Recreational activities, whether structured or unstructured, were always filled with lots of verbal encouragement. The residents encouraged each other. When running the mile, the correctional counselors tracked the time and would give words of encouragement to each resident. It didn't matter if the resident was running or walking, the correctional counselors gave the residents motivation through encouragement as they passed by. With this encouragement, especially from the correctional counselors, the residents pushed themselves to improve their mile time. They didn't run because an officer told them that they must. They did it because a correctional counselor encouraged them to do so. The only thing that made residents run faster than the encouragement they received, were the mosquitoes. When the mosquitoes were out, all the women walked or ran faster to avoid the bites.

Chance loved mile run days, although he wasn't allowed to run with the residents in the gym as he couldn't make a turn on the gym floor without wiping out a pile of residents. But come summertime, he knew that every Wednesday was mile run day out on the rec field. It was most definitely his favorite rec activity and he always came in first place unless it was really hot outside. On hot days, he would run a half mile and then lie down in the shade.

The most favorite rec activity was "Wall Ball." This was a game developed and created in a youth program which carried into the trauma program. It was basically indoor volleyball, except part of the game was to play (or hit) any ball bouncing off the wall. The only rule to this game was not to let the ball touch the ground. However, they didn't use a volleyball. Real volleyballs were far too hard to hit in a straight direction for the skill level. Instead, they played with one of those giant, soft to hit 20-inch play balls. They come in all kinds of colors and are usually found in retail stores in a big giant cage in front of the toy isle. If limited athletic ability or poor eyesight are concerns, this is the only kind of ball to use. In addition, if someone gets hit directly in the face, which happened often, no one really got hurt aside from some embarrassment for a swing and a miss of a giant red ball three times the size of your head. This was the only game they kept score in. And they only kept score so they knew when it was time to rotate positions, like in a real game of volleyball. The residents and staff members all loved this game.

Of course, they played softball as well. Despite the difficult day described in the story previously told about Victorious, softball was the lieutenant's favorite game. Softball was limited to the months of good weather months and determined by the number of mosquitoes that were present outside. As such, they played as much as he could get them outside for it.

Another game they played was kickball. A bit more challenging for an older population, but if they had enough people in good shape, they would play this as well. The lieutenant enjoyed throwing the ball at a few of the overly confident residents. The ones who would taunt him before and throughout the game saying, "Mr. Johnson you throw like a girl. Next time, I'll walk the bases, so you have a chance at hitting me."

They played basketball as well. However, this game was appreciated more by the younger, healthier population.

Fitness Class Creates Confidence

Fitness class was held four days a week, for one hour each day. Many residents coming into the program were out of shape, overweight, or just weak from the lack of physical activity. The class focused on yoga and weight training.

> ***Lieutenant:*** "The residents really look forward to the fitness class."
>
> ***Therapist:*** "They love it. They talk about it all the time. So many of these women are physically broken from addictions and the lifestyles they have come from, and a lot of them have body image issues. It's important for them to have the resources necessary to become physically fit."

Lieutenant: "I asked the fitness teacher what he is doing to make such an impact. He said that he provides them with a workout program, but spends most of his time building their confidence. He said what they really need more than anything is for someone to believe in them. This helps them believe in themselves, and that's when they really begin to apply themselves."

Therapist: "Their improved physical fitness shows, but even more important, is their increased confidence in themselves and improved mental health. The fitness teacher also conducts a mindfulness "cool down" closure to the class. This allows the women to slow down their bodies and minds. He encourages them to accept their bodies as they are, and then he has them visualize their bodies positively transforming through appropriate fitness agendas. This strengthens their motivation and increases their patience in their individual fitness programs.

Lieutenant: "Yes, he isn't managing a bootcamp-style fitness program. Each resident has her own fitness program designed around her specific needs based on her health assessment provided by the nurse. This minimizes the risk of injury; no one has exceeded their workout to the point of injury. The fitness teacher takes on the coaching and confidence-builder role in support of the residents, as opposed to a military drill instructor role."

Health and Medical Makes a Big Difference

Riverside employed one nurse to provide the individual medical care for all its residents. She managed their medications, assessed their fitness capabilities, and provided regular health evaluations, and check-ins as needed. Due to the lifestyles many of the women had endured, their bodies were "worn" down, and many had poor dental hygiene with lots of missing teeth or few teeth at all.

> ***Lieutenant:*** "Another resident has returned from the dentist. She got her dentures. She looks like a different person and is acting like a different person as well. I don't think I ever saw her smile before today. Now, she has a permanent smile on her face."
>
> ***Therapist:*** "So many women have lost teeth to their addictions. But, just as many have lost teeth from being victims of domestic violence. A woman's appearance has a huge effect on her self-confidence. Having bad teeth can hinder a woman's search for a job, engage in a loving relationship, and even keeps them from wanting to leave their house. Having their teeth fixed is extremely important when addressing trauma and reintegrating women back into the community."
>
> ***Lieutenant:*** "The nurse really implements a "trauma informed and responsive" approach to her medical care. I often see her meeting privately with residents. They always feel like their health concerns have been acknowledged."
>
> ***Therapist:*** "She is very respectful of the history of each resident. Many of the women have expressed they do not feel judged by her. She understands "trauma-informed" naturally. She told me once that when a person is labeled as a criminal or inmate or offender, that removes the human aspect of the individual."

"This is the first time I feel like I was treated like a human being. I've been trying to get someone to listen to me about this pain for two years before arriving at Riverside. I'm so grateful for the nurse. I feel like I can smile at the world now."

Resident Testimony

The education program was primarily focused on helping residents to pass their High School Equivalency Test (HISET®).[25] Assistance was also provided in researching and applying for colleges, for those interested. The fitness teacher also led the education program. He had a Bachelor of Science Degree in secondary education, was endorsed in the broad fields of social science, health and physical education, and special education. The education program was created to meet the needs of each resident. The residents in need of HISET testing were administered preliminary practice tests to assess their current education level. He would then tailor the assignments and work independently with each resident until they were ready to take the HISET exam. As with all staff working in the facility, he too, adopted the trauma-informed and responsive relationship-based rapport with his students.

> ***Lieutenant:*** "I heard that another resident has passed her HISET exam. It's nice to see them pass after working so hard for it."
>
> ***Therapist:*** "She is extremely excited about passing the exam. I remember in the beginning she said, 'I won't be able to pass it, I'm too stupid.' I wish you could've seen her facial expression when she learned that she really did pass."
>
> ***Lieutenant:*** "I do see it. She's bouncing off the walls with excitement and pride on the housing unit. I've never seen her so happy. It amazes me how the teacher can get his students to come such a long way in their education, in such a short amount of time."
>
> ***Therapist:*** "He is great about meeting the residents where they are and without judgement. He takes the time to build trust with them."

---

25 Highschool Equivalency Test (HISET)® https://www.google.com/search?q=HISET&rlz=1C1GCEA_enUS828US846&oq=HISET&aqs=chrome..69i57j0l7.3716j0j7&sourceid=chrome&ie=UTF-8

Lieutenant: "He told me they are all intelligent, but they have often been told of their failures so they lack self-confidence. He helps to rebuild their confidence by believing in them before they will believe in themselves. He said he has assumed a cheerleader role with them first, then he teaches them the curriculum."

Therapist: "He understands being trauma-informed and why it is imperative to the educational program."

"I made it! I made it! Because of Riverside I got my HISET. I can't believe I am going to college."
Resident Testimony

Parenting Class

Many of the women were completely overwhelmed by the court-ordered mandates they were responsible to address. Riverside recognized this and offered avenues to reduce some of the associated stress. Parenting classes were offered for those with mandated court orders, or anyone who wanted to attend. Many residents took advantage of this. Contracted facilitators led the parenting classes.

Lieutenant: "It's nice to see so many residents volunteering to attend the parenting class."

Therapist: "They really like it. They are learning things that they were never taught growing up. One resident expressed how she was going to apply the knowledge to both her grandchildren and her adult children."

Lieutenant: "Yes, and I'm glad to see residents who haven't even had children who taking advantage of this class."

Therapist: "Me too. They will learn so much and remember it when they do have children."

Lieutenant: "I would think the teachings will help prevent a lot of child abuse."

Therapist: "It will certainly help. It teaches patience and understanding human growth, development stages and appropriate expectations."

Lieutenant: "It sounds like a really good class."

Therapist: "It's a great class, I'm glad we have it."

"For the first time in my life, I believe I can be a good mother."
Resident Testimony

Progress Meetings Heal

Each week, progress meetings were held for residents who were approximately halfway through their program. This was their opportunity to talk about their progress. They always spoke first. The staff in attendance would then share their assessment of the resident's progress.

Residents would share how the program was working for them and gave feedback as to what they liked and disliked about the program. The team members always asked them two standard questions, "What are your strengths?" and, "What would you change about the program to improve it?" The team members did their best to consider and implement what residents knew they needed.

The residents' input was implemented in a variety of ways. Mostly, it didn't change things for them, but rather for the women soon to follow. The team implemented their suggestions whenever they could, without breaking policy.

After adding coffee to the unit, allowing make-up to be available in the canteen, installing cloth curtains on the room windows for privacy, and no longer requiring residents to ask for personal hygiene products, along with a few other changes, it only took seven months before the women started saying, "Nothing, please don't change anything."

The team always gave feedback that focused on the resident's strengths. They told them what they did well. They gave examples of how they demonstrated goodness.

Therapist

Progress meetings were held every Tuesday at two o'clock. The events that occurred in the progress meetings provided me with great insight about the women, and so much more. I felt absolutely honored to gain insight from my co-workers. They were genuine, sincere, heartfelt, and positive. They were caring and motivationally truthful. They not only recognized the women as being very human, they connected with them, and it was easily felt throughout the room. The internal progress that each woman revealed brought on a swelling of positive emotion that would often result in a release through their tears. These tears were not engulfed in sadness or regret, they were engulfed in the most positive of emotions and everyone in the room experienced them, not just the residents.

I did not deny mine, nor did I announce them. The male staff never cried, they "leaked." "I'm not crying, my eyes leak," or "It's a medical thing, quit looking at me," they would say. Sometimes the emotion was released in the voice box. I could not have felt more pride to be among them all. We all belonged exactly where we were. No one in the progress meetings could deny the healing.

During progress meetings, I could always pick out SAMHSA's Key Principles of a Trauma-Informed Approach.[26]

Although the women started their individual progress meeting with great nervousness, all of them left with a feeling of *safety*. All of the staff felt safe and we all looked forward to the progress meetings. The women felt *empowered* when some of their suggestions became a reality. The staff expressed *transparency and trustworthiness,* and often received statements from the women indicating, they too, felt the same. Mostly, there was *collaboration and mutuality* expressed in both verbal and non-verbal ways. *Cultural, historical, and gender issues* were expressed as strengths and the healing was insurmountable. Many times, there was a promotion of *peer support* right before and after the progress meetings.

I quickly learned to love Tuesdays at 2 o'clock.

Chemical Dependency Treatment

Chemical Dependency (CD) treatment is directly and indirectly related to trauma. Both CD treatment and trauma treatment are essential components to recovery within the correctional system. Riverside's CD treatment program consisted of group counseling and individual sessions. Each resident would attend group counseling twice a week, and meet individually with the CD counselor, as needed. Individual sessions and group sessions were held off the housing unit in either the therapist's or CD counselor's office.

In group sessions, the women shared their addictions and learned how their addictions correlated to the trauma in their lives. As they identified and began dealing with the trauma they had experienced, they learned how this led to self-medication. In turn, they began to shed feelings of guilt and shame. They studied their triggers and urges, and developed relapse

---

26 Substance Abuse and Mental Health Services Administration (SAMHSA)© https://www.samhsa.gov.

prevention plans to overcome their feelings to use. Sometimes, in a mock session, they would practice saying 'no' to potential friends and drug dealers. Principally, they focused on their strengths and learned how to exert power over their addiction.

Lieutenant: "Why do the CD and trauma treatment groups take place off the housing unit? Why don't we hold these groups in the dayroom of the housing unit?"

Therapist: "The residents need a psychological break from addressing specialized treatment, such as addictions and trauma. If the group and/or individual sessions are held in their living space, they may not feel the break, and as a result, they may have lingering emotions that continue the thoughts of what went on in the group. In essence, they may not get the psychological break and feeling that 'it' (trauma) can rest while they take care of themselves."

Lieutenant: "I can understand this. It's like leaving work-related stress at work and not dragging it home. How can trauma result in a person becoming addicted to drugs?"

Therapist: "I can give a couple of examples:

She was nervous but excited. The day had come, the labor pains were five minutes apart, and her baby boy was about to arrive. She was young, in her early twenties, but she wanted and needed someone to love.

She had people in her life that she loved dearly, her mom and her husband. But she longed to have this little one in her life for years before it would become a reality. She remembered crying on her husband's shoulders every month when she would get her period. She thought something was wrong with her, that God had kept her from getting pregnant. But, today was the day that would all change.

The pain was incredible. The contractions were coming fast and hard. Finally, her baby boy was out, and the pain was all but gone. The doctor's expression immediately dropped. She still remembers him stuttering, almost whispering...

The room was suddenly very busy with many more nurses and other people wearing white coats. Then, it was all a big blur. She heard something about his color not being right, and he was not breathing. Then she heard the nurse say, "I can't find a heartbeat." Lastly, she heard something about "still born." Three weeks later, she used drugs for the first time."

> ***Lieutenant:*** "In this case, it's easy for me to see this woman, whoever she is, is not simply using drugs because she has no regard for the law or the people in her life. She is self-medicating because she did not have the treatment to provide positive coping skills in response to this traumatic experience. Having this information makes it difficult to see a person like this as a renegade criminal."

> ***Therapist:*** "Yes, I agree. She's not a criminal. She's using to make the emotional pain go away. Another example is:

She joined the military to serve her country. At the time, there were only but a few women enlisted in the military. The men she was surrounded by had difficulty accepting females serving side by side with them. She endured sexist comments and sexually harassing statements. She did not immediately report them as she had hoped the men would come around.

One weekend, she was invited to an 'off-base party'. She was happy for the invite and hopeful it meant she was finally being accepted. Instead, she was gang-raped for several hours by many of the men at the party. During the rape, she was repeatedly told things like, "this is what women were made for". The rape left her unable to ever give birth. Her body was damaged beyond repair.

She remained sober for the following 18 months of her court hearings and testimony where she relived the trauma at every turn. She kept telling herself, "I am strong enough to see this through for the sake of all of the women to follow." She won the lawsuit. Her settlement from the government was significant, but it did not erase the memories nor reduce the lingering nightmares. She began using drugs almost immediately after the court process."

> ***Lieutenant:*** "They gave her money as compensation for her trauma. Maybe enough to make her go away, but not enough to help her trauma go away."
>
> ***Therapist:*** "Addiction crosses all spectrums: economic, race, gender. You are absolutely right. Money won't keep a person from becoming addicted. In more cases than not, if you address the trauma, you can treat the addiction."

"I'm leaving Riverside, and this is the first time I have ever left a treatment program,when I don't already have a plan to use."
Resident Testimony

Treating Trauma

Trauma treatment was the primary focus of Riverside's program. The trauma therapist conducted group sessions twice a week and individualized sessions each week for all of the residents. Both group sessions and individual sessions were held off the housing unit in the therapist's office.

The trauma treatment exposed horrendous emotional pain and experiences. The treatment agenda was to acknowledge the trauma, clear it by addressing it, and ultimately releasing it. This was often an excruciating and seemingly unbearable process.

In group sessions, the women acquired strength from each other to share their experiences. Together, they acknowledged their traumatic experiences with full support from their peers. This formed the bond which would grow into a foundation of support.

In the individualized therapy sessions, the therapist worked with each resident to begin the unique and independent process to clear trauma from their subconscious.

The final step in the treatment program was the process of letting it go. A final step in the treatment program, but not to be mistaken with the final step in recovery. Recovery from trauma can be a long process without treatment. The 'letting go ceremony' was intended to significantly reduce the impact of trauma on the residents. Together again in their group setting, the women learned to let it go.

> ***Lieutenant:*** "I'm trying to understand more of what these women are dealing with when it comes to their trauma. It's extremely difficult to understand without knowing at least what the overall trauma is. What kind of trauma are we dealing with?"
>
> ***Therapist:*** "I recognize how difficult this is for you and your staff. I appreciate and understand your need for information. I can give you a couple of common examples of trauma related to this population. I can't connect the trauma with a specific resident. If I did, I would be breaching confidentiality, but here is a common scenario.

One woman went looking for meth. She had been using consistently every day for the past week. She was coming down, and her brain and body was screaming for more. Although her drug friend had warned her never to go there, that day she was desperate. She had never shot up before. This was the first time she allowed a needle in her arm.

She woke up in a haze. She could feel that she was still a little high. She felt sick. The thought of vomiting filled her mouth with saliva. Her head hurt bad. She not only wondered what time it was, she wondered what day it was.

The flashes of blurred memories came at her fast, glimpses of horror. Her heart started pounding rapidly. She tried to get up, but her right arm was restrained. When her blurred vision focused, she saw the handcuffs and panicked. She started crying. She started begging, 'please let me go, please.'

She pleaded, 'I will do anything you want, please let me go.' He came at her with a needle, a 'rig'. She yelled, 'No, not anymore, I've had enough, please don't.' He forced the needle into her arm and after the initial jolt, oddly, she felt better. The room slowly darkened.

Addiction and the process of looking for drugs is a dangerous world. Many times, the people, both women and men, often get much more than the drug they are looking for. 'The more strung out you are, the more preyed upon you become. It's like people can just tell you're an easy target. 'My mother is right, I deserved what I got.'"

> ***Lieutenant:*** "As terrible of a story as this is, there are many people who will suggest the mother in this story has a point. This woman, whoever she is, did in fact, seek out drugs in a dangerous place despite her friend's warning. Some people will say she caused her own traumatic experience. I think this is one reason we have a correctional system which lacks empathy for the addictions and traumas criminals have."

> ***Therapist:*** "It boils down to the quick judgement of others. We need to get past the 'why' aspect of this. What would happen in the local emergency room if every doctor first decided to judge why the patient had a gunshot wound? Did he instigate it? Should we lower our standard of treatment because he shouldn't have had a gun in the first place? Or, he shouldn't have been hunting with that gun? Or, he was drinking at the time he was

shot, and therefore, he shouldn't get the same care? Our judgment of others interferes with our treatment process.

Another example is a woman and her boyfriend had been consistently using drugs for over two weeks. They were driving to another town to find more drugs. Both had absconded. Neither of them had checked in with their parole officers. They had scattered plans of getting married. The truth is, they were too high to implement any of it. She remembered the radio in the car was playing and they were both singing and laughing at themselves when suddenly, he shouted cuss words and grabbed the rearview mirror.

She remembers him screaming, 'I'm not going back, I will not go back!' She knew what that meant because they had talked about it so many times before. Still, she wasn't prepared for what happened next.

He sped the car up fast and then she heard the police sirens and saw the flashing lights. They were now on a high-speed chase. Her heart was pounding like never before. This was not going to end well. More police cars joined the chase. He screamed, 'we are not going to make it.' Then he slammed on the brakes, stopped the car and pulled out his gun.

She pleaded with him, 'Please take me with you! Shoot me first! Please don't leave me behind!' He looked at her with an expression she'll never forget. With her sitting right next to him he put the gun in his mouth and pulled the trigger."

Lieutenant: "I don't know what to say. What a horrific experience. How does a person recover from something like this?"

Therapist: "It is a process for sure. I am reluctant to state that a person can fully recover from an experience such as this. It is hard for most people to acknowledge the event. And acknowledging the event requires acceptance of the event. Many of the residents struggle to accept what has happened to them. The group treatment process really helps because the residents hear similar stories from others. They aren't alone in the trauma. That, in itself, is a powerful step towards recovery."

Lieutenant: "I want to believe people can recover from a trauma such as this, but I don't imagine they would ever forget it. So, recovery from trauma must be about learning how to live with the memory as opposed to forgetting it? I can see how a person without help in dealing with the trauma would choose to self-medicate with drugs."

Therapist: "You are exactly right. It is about living with a memory without re-experiencing the memory as if it is happening all over again. It is an individualized process. There are techniques that can help the subconscious mind recall the event without the triggering details of the event."

Lieutenant: "Clearly, it's a difficult path for anyone to take. I would imagine in this case, she would have a host of triggers related to the experience, such as the song they sang, the police sirens, the sound of the gun shot, the car, the area in which the incident took place, obviously the boyfriend, and many more. What are some of the techniques used to manage these triggers?"

Therapist: "There are a number of common therapeutic approaches to help the healing process of trauma.[27] Pharmacotherapy is one, using medication to manage invasive reactions or nightmares. Behavior therapy, more commonly known as exposure therapy, is another. Psychodynamic therapy is yet another. There are more, but here at Riverside, I am using individualized and group therapy."

---

27 Common therapy approaches to help the healing process of trauma. (2011) https://www.google.com/search?q=trauma+techniques+therapy&oq=trauma+tcchni&aqs=chrome.5.0j69i57j0l6.9886j0j7&sourceid=chrome&ie=UTF-8

"I have never known a person so selfless and loving as my trauma therapist. You always reminded me to love myself."
Resident Testimony

The "Letting Go" Ceremony

The Letting Go ceremony was simply optional for the residents to attend as there were no credits given for attending. There were no sanctions given for not attending. This was voluntary and not required in order to graduate. The ceremony was held at least once during a resident's stay. The purpose was to provide an opportunity for residents to acknowledge, make peace with, and let go of their trauma. For weeks, the women had been preparing letters that no one would ever receive. Instead, the letters would be burned at the end of the ceremony. The letters revealed the burdens the women had been trying to run from. Today was the day they might speak of the events they previously took an oath of silence on. Most of the women spoke of the traumas that haunted their subconscious mind to the point of changing behavior without conscience permission.

The therapist gathered her strength and prayers as she apprehensively prepared the room. This day would weigh heavily on her spiritually, emotionally and physically. Ceremony days left her feeling completely exhausted.

Many of the staff who gathered the courage to participate, were affected as well. The transportation officer attended one time only. She left early that day with a migraine promising never to attend again. The next day, she stated, "No wonder they all ended up in addiction or prison. It's really not completely their fault. I felt so honored to be there and hear their stories. I will never look at them again with the same judgement. I cried myself to sleep last night thinking about what these women have had to endure."

During the ceremony, the women would reset their spirits and gain a new perspective about themselves. The sharing of their stories would bring a sense of unity, knowing that they weren't alone in the darkest of spaces, would bring its own light.

They all filed into the spiritual room, everyone, the women from both sides of the housing unit, staff who chose to attend, and two correctional counselors who were mandated to attend. They slowly entered the room where soft music was playing. Pillows were placed in a circle on the floor, with some chairs intertwined for those whose bodies were too beaten to sit on the floor comfortably.

The music was quieted, the only sound was breathing. A sense of nervousness filled the room as the women settled. A bowl of sweetgrass and sage was passed around the circle for those who chose to cleanse themselves. The softest sound emerged in the room, gaining momentum and intensity. Together, a young resident and the case manager sang 'Amazing Grace' while the smudging continued. An abalone shell, gifted by the ocean, carried the smoldering aroma of sweetgrass and sage. For the therapist, it was a powerful moment.

Therapist

"As it was passed to me, I felt reverent and loved as I too welcomed the smudge. I asked the Great Spirit to help me stay on the sacred path while I smudged my feet. I asked to be reminded to bend with life's bumps as the smudge reached my knees. As I raised the braid of sweetgrass towards my hips and abdomen, I asked for balance in all my endeavors, and the ability to receive joy. My heartbeat slowed when the smoke reached it. I thanked the Great Spirit for all the love I felt towards others, and I asked to be reminded to reach out with love in my future connections. When the smudge reached my face, I asked that the words that would leave my mouth stay honest and true. And when the smudge reached my eyes and forehead, I requested to always see the beauty in people and to think positively about them. Above all, I asked to stay connected to the Great Spirit."

Ribbons had been laid on the ceramic dish intentionally placed in the center of the room.

By choosing a ribbon, the participants would invite their greatest supporter, living or not, to join them in spirit, and to help them let go of the hurt of the past.

I was so grateful for the fitness teacher who always attended. He had great insight on the healing that took place during this ceremony. He also had his own trauma that he was willing to process, share and release. He would begin the ceremony, allowing the women to be a part of his healing, as well as letting them see that he too was very human, and they were not alone in the murky waters of residual trauma. He lent them the courage to sputter the words they had written in anguish during the previous days.

On my left, the first resident chose a purple ribbon and asked her grandmother to join them as she sobbed her story:

> "Dear grandma, please help me forgive your son as I read this letter: I was so scared being only ten years old when he took me to that dark house and sold me to his friends so he could get his bag of dope… I have a hard time understanding why I'm the one in prison and he is not…"

When she finished reading her letter, she tied her ribbon to the ribbon her peer was nervously holding. This part of the ceremony allowed the next woman sitting in the circle to know it was now her turn, as well as to remind them that they were all connected. Then, the next woman spoke:

> "Dear uncle, I am trying to forgive you for molesting me all those years. I finally made the connection after I learned what Grandpa did to you, but it still hurts that you did it to me…"

> "Dear ex-boyfriend, I still can't wrap my brain around the fact that you shook him to his death. I went to work that day trusting you with my three-year-old son…"

The circle slowly continued, as their traumas were spoken out loud, in many cases, for the first time ever.

> "Dear Sister, it's been fifteen years. I am trying to let go of the anger I have toward you for stealing my husband away from me and my three children. They grew up without a dad and without their aunt, and it tore our entire family apart. Mom still begs me to forgive you…"

Each resident would pick a colored ribbon from the ceramic dish and speak of their secret story. Those who wanted would read some or all of the letter they had spent a lifetime creating. Each story revealed a horrifying event that brought tears to all who shared in the pain.

> "Dear mom, I was only twelve when you shot me up for the first time stating, 'This will make you feel better'…"

> "Dear boyfriend, you were the love of my life. I do not understand why you did it. I can't get the image out of my head of your lifeless body. I have been afraid to fall asleep ever since that morning..."

> "Dear dad, you put my mom in the hospital because you beat her so badly. She will never be the same, and neither will I. How am I supposed to forgive you for taking our mom away? All of us kids were placed in foster care homes…"

Finding forgiveness for others is difficult. Finding forgiveness for self is often nearly impossible.

> "Dear mom, I tried my best to take care of my little brother, I felt like he was more my kid than yours. I have a hard time forgiving myself for letting him drown in the lake that day. I know I was only nine years old, but I still feel like it was my fault…"

> "Dear brother, I judged you so harshly over your drug addiction. I did not know that my act of 'tough love' and kicking you out of my house would end with you freezing to death that cold winter night. I am addicted myself now, and I get so angry that my husband won't kick me out of his life, I don't deserve to be alive..."

> "Dear drug dealer, I went to get dope from you, not to get tied up and raped by every slime bag friend you invited over..."

The room filled with sorrow, shock, anger and despair. The sniffling and whimpering and blowing of noses would fade into the background as the next person fought back the tears and forced the words to move from the dark pit deep within the soul, up the throat, and at last, be spat into the atmosphere, completely surrounded by nonjudgmental safety and backed by a common love based in understanding and unity.

The hardest letters to hear were the ones that started, 'dear son' or 'dear daughter.' The women who had neglected or abused their children were riddled with such an intense guilt that it kept them in an addictive state of perpetual use. They desperately needed an avenue to rid themselves of negative feelings they had about themselves and start to reframe the past. Each woman hoped to see herself as a person who could get better. However, the release of such despairing issues brought on a catharsis for everyone in the room.

> "Dear sweet little baby girl, it's time to forgive myself and I don't know how. I did not hold your hand while we crossed the street that day. I believe if I just would have held your hand, you might still be with me..."

> "Dear daughter, please forgive me for leaving you with the babysitter time and time again. I should not have believed her

> over your crying for me not to leave you. She beat you to your death, and I feel it's all my fault…"
>
> "Dear son, I was driving drunk the day we crashed the car. I should be the one in a comatose state, not you…"
>
> "Dear baby boy, I am so sorry for leaving you in the hot car while I went into the dealer's house to get my fix. I was too selfishly high to realize the time that had passed. Now, you are with grandma, I robbed you of your whole life and God won't let me die..."
>
> "Dear grandma, you were the only one in my life that cared for me and helped me whenever I needed you. I am so sorry for stealing everything from you. I know it's my fault that you had to go to a nursing home because I wiped out your bank account…"

I remember the shame and guilt expressed by one particular resident when preparing for this ceremony.

> "How can I even pretend to forgive myself for leaving my baby in his crib until his head became flat. I don't deserve to be a mother, that's why I don't have him."

And another resident anguished,

> "I put my little sister in his bed so he wouldn't do it to me. How can I forgive myself? I was supposed to protect her!"

After all those in attendance who chose to share out loud the secrets they had individually buried for so long, they headed outside to the medicine wheel to burn their letters and release their burdens. The walk from the medicine wheel where the letters were burned to the gym where they replenished and celebrated their new freedom carried a special magic - a supernatural healing and unforeseen lightheartedness. The burden of carrying deep dark secrets for all those years had been lifted. The release carried a physical, psychological and spiritual blessing. The women looked younger and brighter. They were connected, no longer alone. The staff saw the women through softer and more understanding eyes. Once in the mezzanine, they ate fruit of all kinds, drank coffee, and shared their support of each other. Both staff and residents were just people that day, people whose hearts were lifted from heaviness. Everyone had let go of something. When we let go of things in a way the subconscious understands, the iceberg beneath starts to settle, as does the physical nervous system. The Letting Go Ceremony provided the perfect outlet to make that happen."

"I have always been scared to talk about my past and feelings,but I have learned how to let it go."
Resident Testimony

Safety & Security Without Power and Control

Throughout the trauma program's existence, there were only two 'use-of-force' incidents. Although, the severity in the incidents were so minor, they should not be classified as a "use-of-force." Both incidents involved verbal disputes between residents. In both cases, the correctional counselors gave verbal redirects to the residents to stop their confrontation. However, because the residents did not stop, the correctional counselor placed a hand on the resident's arm and walked her away from the scene. This action stopped the disruptive behavior and stopped the dispute from escalating. However, simply because a correctional counselor placed a hand on a resident, the incident was classified as a use-of-force.

Other than these minor incidents, no use-of-force was required to restrain a resident to the ground. No cell extraction was ever needed. No hand cuffs or soft restraints were ever used. Not one physical fight between residents occurred. Not one resident attempted to escape. No tattooing was conducted. Nothing from the therapist's office was ever used as a weapon, or even used inappropriately for that matter.

Throughout the duration of the program, not one strip search was conducted. Not one weapon was ever made or used to harm anyone. The facility conducted random urine drug testing, and not one resident ever tested positive for an illegal drug.

> ***Therapist:*** "I just received an email from the administrator. Guess what our numbers are?"
>
> ***Lieutenant:*** "I've never received an email from the administrator. What are the numbers?"
>
> ***Therapist:*** "71.4 percent successfully remained in the community for longer than 90 days! I don't think Montana has ever had numbers that good."
>
> ***Lieutenant:*** "That's a 28.6 percent recidivism rate!!! That's astonishing. And we accomplished that with a relatively short program, as compared to other treatment programs. The taxpayers will be proud of the Montana Department of Corrections when they find out we are reducing recidivism."
>
> ***Therapist:*** "Yes they will, and we accomplished it in one third of the time compared to other treatment facilities, within or contracted by the department. It triples the success."
>
> ***Lieutenant:*** "Was 90 days the only review they conducted?"
>
> ***Therapist:*** "No. They also ran numbers that showed over 66 percent remained in the community longer than six months, and almost 64 percent have remained in the community longer than a year. We really do have a phenomenal program!"

Lieutenant: "That is mind blowing in comparison to most recidivism rates! We are doing something right for sure."

The People Who Made It Work

The success of a program is often attributed to administrative policies and procedures written for the program. This was not the case at Riverside. The fact is, there weren't many policies and procedures in place when the program started, and not many written by the time it ended. The program at Riverside was a pilot project. This was unique and, in a way, attributed to its success. It was not an easy process for the staff to immediately adapt to such a different treatment culture. It took time. Yet, every single staff, in some small way, had contributed to its creation and had everything to do with its successful implementation.

It is not uncommon to find barriers between treatment staff and security staff, especially in a correctional setting. The lieutenant and the therapist had experienced the negative effects of working in a divisive program throughout their careers. The lieutenant had experienced barriers existing between the treatment, educational, and the security staff. The therapist had experienced similar barriers in the mental health field.

These barriers often create a hardship and prevent unity of the facility's common goals. There are many components of working in a 24-hour facility that require the teamwork of both treatment specialists and all other staff members. In a treatment focused facility, the treatment specialists can inadvertently minimize the contributing role of the other staff. The therapist was adamant this would not be the case at Riverside. The lieutenant was adamant this would not be the case at Riverside. They both had such strong beliefs and determination for this, they were able to see beyond their differences to unite the treatment and security elements.

They were prepared for their different perspectives, and they were resolute to see both the treatment and security needs implemented in unity, with respect.

The lieutenant and the therapist had found a way to not only respect each other's roles, but also to understand and value the importance of being united with the entire team.

Riverside's unique teamwork and transparency amongst staff members greatly influenced the success of the facility's common goal of implementing trauma-informed treatment, while simultaneously maintaining a safe and secure environment.

The credit to the success of the program belongs to the hard work and flexibility of all who worked there. This included everyone from the superintendent, to the receptionist, and everyone in between who had accepted the challenge to implement a treatment culture in a correctional setting.

> ***Therapist:*** "I am so grateful that many of the staff had worked with the youth population prior to this program. I can't imagine that we would have had much success if it wasn't for the previous administration fostering the relationship-based rapport in the youth program. This culture was further perfected by the correctional counselors in the trauma program."

> ***Lieutenant:*** "Yes, I think you're right. The correctional counselor role previously established provided a foundation of skills to facilitate groups and engage in the residents' programming. This was imperative to the successful transition. Correctional counselors further advanced the therapeutic relationship-based rapport despite opposing direction from prison and jail officer trainings. It was the individual characteristics of each correctional counselor, their dedication, loyalty, and professionalism, which mounted the treatment program's success."

Therapist: "Our chemical dependency counselors tailored their treatment to support the trauma the women were addressing. That, in turn, supported the trauma aspects of the program."

Lieutenant: "Our case managers did an outstanding job in tailoring the intake process by welcoming residents, speaking to them in a non-authoritative manner, thoroughly explaining the expectations and consequences, and encouraging residents to ask questions. In addition, they managed their caseloads in a timely manner and remained transparent throughout the process."

Therapist: "Our receptionist was the face of the program. She provided the first impression to all who entered the facility. Her 'southern hospitality' was so natural and effective. She welcomed every resident as a human being and never judged them."

Lieutenant: "The fitness teacher was a perfect fit for the residents. He maintained healthy boundaries with the women, and balanced his role as a teacher with structure, compassion, empathy, and humor. He believed in the women first. This allowed them to believe in themselves."

Therapist: "We couldn't have picked a better transportation and training officer. She made sure the residents heard the best music every chance she could, and it was usually rock and roll. She was free-spirited about dancing and singing too. The women were always laughing when they were with her.

Lieutenant: "Our maintenance man had a similar influence, always smiling and never seemed stressed. Nothing seemed to shake him up despite routinely working on something that was broken. The rec field was maintained and groomed like a golf course."

Therapist: "Our compliance specialist was an advocate for the residents. He was always sending the most useful articles my way. He had an uncanny ability to predict when I needed resources to support the women's rights, and made sure that I had them."

Lieutenant: "Our nurse was a nurse above all nurses. They simply do not come with a bigger heart and passion and compassion to provide medical care."

Therapist: "Well stated. I would have said those very words."

Lieutenant: "Our superintendent was also unmatched. I have the utmost respect for him. I truly believe the program would never have gotten off the ground without his courage to re-evaluate policies and procedures. He fought battles for the program, which were sometimes out of sight from the rest of us. I know he fought hard for the residents and the program."

Therapist: "Our superintendent was the absolute perfect person for the job at the right time. I loved that he often sat and ate the same lunch with the residents. In the progress meetings, he often acknowledged how the environments the women were raised in had influenced their criminal behavior. Many times, he shared his gratitude for his caring parents who actively participated in his upbringing. He often stated, 'I could be on the other side of my job if it weren't for my parents.' I think he understood how an environment can affect a person's behavior. He endured a lot of hardship defending our program. I will be forever grateful for him. I know I speak for us both when I say we wish him and all the staff the best of what life has to offer."

Lieutenant: "The program simply would not have been the success it was if it weren't for all of the staff. It was unequivocally the people who made it work."

"When I arrived, I was a beaten shell of a woman. You welcomed me with kindness, giving, insight, intelligence and comfort, and I could go on and on. I won't ever forget this place and all the people who have taught me so much."

Resident Testimony

CHAPTER FIVE

The Closure of Riverside
A Hint from A Newspaper Article

On June 19, 2018, a news article posted in the Montana Standard newspaper titled, "A big break in the program: Elkhorn Treatment Center population drops by nearly half".[28]

Elkhorn Treatment Center[29] (ETC) is a 47-bed residential treatment-based correctional facility located across the street from the Riverside trauma treatment program. The ETC serves 42 females under contract and custody of the Montana Department of Corrections. The therapist shared the article with the lieutenant.

> ***Therapist:*** "I think you should read this article. It points out that ETC's nine-month substance abuse and addiction treatment program rely heavily on their population numbers for its successful treatment. A resident is quoted in the article suggesting that 80 percent of treatment comes from her peers. She said,

---

28 McDermott, Ted. "'*A Big Break in the Program*': *Elkhorn Treatment Center Population Drops by Nearly Half*." Montana Standard. June 19, 2018. https://mtstandard.com/news/local/a-big-break-in-the-program-elkhorn-treatment-center-population-drops-by-nearly-half/article_58955590-f841-50ac-82c0-8df269e9d536.html

29 https://www.boydandrew.com/services/elkhorn/

'the higher the numbers, the better feedback you get'. The article goes on to explain that their numbers dropped nearly in half."

Lieutenant: "The Chief Executive Officer (CEO) of Boyd Andrew Community Services, (the organization which owns and operates ETC) is quoted as saying, 'When the referrals go away, the bills don't go away, the operating costs do not go away. So, it's really harmful on our budget'."

Therapist: "Right. And look at this, DOC communications director states, 'referrals to Elkhorn have declined as a result of an increase in referrals to the Riverside Recovery and Reentry Program.' That statement worries me, something is going on."

Lieutenant: "Privatized centers contracted with the Department of Corrections depend on the department to send them referrals for their programs. This is how they cover the expenses for their program and facility. Each incarcerated person has a cost per day attached to them. I wouldn't worry about it. See right here. The article says the CEO is going to meet with the Department of Corrections next week. I'm sure the department will resolve this."

The Department's Solution

On September 25, 2018, roughly three months after the news article was written, the superintendent of Riverside informed all of the staff members that there would be a meeting the next day. The meeting would be facilitated by the director of DOC, the deputy director, and other administrative personnel. Everyone felt a little nervousness as they all pondered what the meeting would be about. The therapist was on vacation, and therefore was not in attendance.

The next day, on September 26, 2018, the director and approximately half a dozen other DOC central office staff arrived at Riverside. The majority of the staff at Riverside attended the meeting when the director announced, "Inmates in the 25-bed infirmary, currently held in Lewistown, Montana, would be moved to the Riverside correctional facility." He further stated, "the decision to close the Lewistown facility and repurpose the Riverside correctional facility was driven by budget deficits and operational needs." Furthermore, "Montana has two DOC-contracted women's treatment facilities and there was inadequate population to support a third program." The administrative team also announced that three positions from Riverside would be eliminated. Those positions included the superintendent, the lieutenant, and the case manager. All other staff would be retained with possible position transfers to other facilities. The twenty-two women currently in the Riverside program would be placed in the community for treatment, or moved to a contracted treatment program by October 9.

Approximately a week after the all-staff meeting, the therapist returned from her vacation.

> ***Lieutenant:*** "Hello Rhonda. A lot has happened while you were gone."
>
> ***Therapist:*** "I heard they closed the program. I can't tell you how shocked and sad I feel about this."
>
> ***Lieutenant:*** "I would have called you, but I didn't want to deliver news like this on your birthday."
>
> ***Therapist:*** "Thank you. That would have definitely negatively impacted my birthday. I need to meet with all of the women, it's important that we help them process this decision."
>
> ***Lieutenant:*** "More than half of them are already gone."
>
> ***Therapist:*** "What do you mean they are gone, what does that mean, gone where?"

Lieutenant: "The ones who were near completion were discharged to their homes in the community. The others are still here."

Therapist: "Oh my God, was there any closure for the women who left? Did they get any referrals for treatment service in their community?"

Lieutenant: "I'm not sure about referrals for services, but yes, we made sure that each resident had a rock ceremony. It was rushed, but we made sure every resident had one specifically related to each individual."

Therapist: "I am so grateful you saw to that, but I'm so angry right now. I need to be able to provide closure for them. It's irresponsible and unethical to drop services without properly referring and assuring that my clients are clinically ready to transition. I could lose my license if I did something like this in my private practice. I can't explain how damaging this is from an ethical treatment perspective. I am furious!"

Lieutenant: "I understand your frustration. I'm concerned about my correctional counselors as well. They were told that they could accept the lay-off, or be reassigned to the state penitentiary in Deer Lodge Montana, or work at the Lewistown facility until it closes on December 1 . Round-trip to Deer Lodge is a three-hour commute from here. The commute to Lewistown is eight hours, round-trip. The worst part is that they only have less than two weeks to make their decisions."

Therapist: "I'm so sorry this is happening. I know a few of them are single parents and have children that can't be left alone. You are one of them Michael, how is this going to affect you?"

Lieutenant: "Many of my counselors are parents, but regardless of having children, all of them have families, responsibilities, and obligations. None of us were expecting something like this. We are all shocked. None of us expected to be shut down, and now we must make decisions on where we will be working in less than two weeks. We're all just shocked."

Therapist: "How can anyone make decisions like that in less than two weeks? What are your counselors saying about this?"

Lieutenant: "We don't have much of a choice. I've been checking in with as many of my staff as I can. When I asked one counselor how he was doing with the news, he simply looked at me and said, 'Other than that Mrs. Lincoln, how was the play?' All I could do was stare at him knowing the profound reality behind what he had just said. I'm so worried about all of them. And I can't do anything about it."

The lieutenant was overly concerned with the responsibility he felt towards the individual staff members that he had become so close to. He was not recognizing his own trauma. The therapist was overly concerned about the residents, and she too, was not recognizing her trauma.

Therapist: "Please remind the staff that they have the SAMHSA© guidelines of how to deal with this in their pockets. You do understand that all of you are now experiencing trauma on some level. Some more than others, but please know that you and your staff are experiencing trauma. I'm worried about everyone. The more responsible each person feels, the deeper the trauma. I'm worried about you, and you are more worried about your staff. I'm worried about the residents who are already gone, and I need to connect with the residents who are still here. I'm wondering if any of this has sunk in for you on a personal level? How are *you,* Michael?"

Lieutenant: "I just bought a house three months ago. I separated from my wife four months ago. I'm a single parent with a teenager and I just found out I have lost my job after eleven years with the DOC. I am terrified. How are you?"

Therapist: "I'll be fine. I have my private practice to fall back on. I'm angry the department has little to no regard to the effects they are putting on the very people their website states are 'family'. I certainly wouldn't put this trauma on any family member of mine. What about you? Where'd they send you?"

Lieutenant: "I was 'let go,' along with the superintendent and the case manager. All three of us will be laid off this November. The staff in the Human Resources Department have told us they would do all they could to place us throughout the department before November, but they have made no promises."

Therapist: "I'm so sorry. I hope to God they can find you all new positions. I know the superintendent just bought a new truck, and that has to be causing him additional stress. I know the difficult decision of closing programs sometimes needs to happen. What I do not understand is *how* they are going about it. They are showing little regard or consideration for how they are affecting their 'family'."

Lieutenant: "We're all shocked with this news. None of us know what we'll do. How could we? I wish they would have given us more time to make these decisions. I can't imagine the department administration hasn't been debating this outcome for quite some time. Why would they keep it a secret up until now? If they would've just communicated with us and told us that the program was being reviewed for possible closure, all the staff and residents could've better prepared for the outcome. I never would've taken out a loan for a new home."

Therapist: "I wished the department would have openly communicated their plan. It would've saved a lot of people from a lot of trauma. What they've done is like telling a drowning person a life preserver *might* be close by and to tread water while they go look for what *might* or *might* not be there."

Lieutenant: "That about sums it up for me. I feel like I can't breathe. It feels like everyone around me can see that I'm stressed out. I keep telling myself to accept what is happening, but I can't make sense of it. I need to understand this. We've been running a program that is actually helping people and reducing recidivism in half the time of these other treatment centers. Why shut down *this* program?"

Therapist: "What's this I hear about a geriatric population moving here? Why would they move them here?"

Lieutenant: "Hell if I know, it makes absolutely no sense to me. A geriatric population is sure to need medical services, and this facility is 30 miles away from the nearest hospital, and the route includes a mountain pass. The 60-mile round-trip to the nearest hospital is going to cost the taxpayers a fortune."

Therapist: "I agree, it's going to be expensive. Do you know how many times that pass has been closed over the last decade? Just since I've worked here, the mountain pass has been closed at least three times due to the snow or vehicle accidents. What are they going to do when that happens?"

Lieutenant: "They won't be driving a vehicle, that's for sure. I suppose they'll have to forgo the medical treatment, or who knows, get a helicopter or a dog sled."

Therapist: "The unit really isn't set up for men in walkers and wheelchairs."

Lieutenant: "They seem to recognize that. They said they're going to remodel the unit to be more ADA (American Disability Act) compliant."

Therapist: "That'll cost the taxpayers another fortune."

Lieutenant: "That's why they want the residents out so fast, to start the remodeling of the unit. Riverside has the largest recreational gym of all the DOC facilities in Montana. It's even bigger than the gym in the State prisons. Now, the gym is reserved for a population of inmates in wheelchairs and walkers. I just can't make any sense of it."

Therapist: "None of this is making sense. It all seems rushed. Do you remember that article we read three months ago? The one about Elk Horn Treatment Centers number of referrals going down?"

Lieutenant: "I do and that might shed some light behind the closure. Maybe we should look at those contracts."

Therapist: "We should. It's public information."

The Twenty-Year Contract

In an attempt to make some sense of this decision, Michael and Rhonda searched the public domain of information[30] and found the hundreds of contracts that DOC had with private agencies. They then decided to view the twenty-four-page contract[31] between the DOC and Elkhorn Treatment Center (ETC).

30 https://www.mtacdl.org/attachments/CPE/Chico_2015/5_CAmbroseDOCComProg.pdf

31 https://cor.mt.gov/Portals/104/Resources/Contracts/Boyd%20Andrew%2007-016-ACCD%20thru%20Amend%205.pdf?ver=2020-01-29-114505-933

Michael: "Oh my God, it's a twenty-year contract beginning April 9, 2007, and not ending until April 8, 2027.

Rhonda: "Twenty years, seriously, twenty years? Who agrees to a twenty-year contract?"

Michael: "It says here that the legislators agreed to it. The question is, why would legislators commit to a twenty-year contract?"

Rhonda: "Holy cow, ETC is getting over two million dollars each year. That's 40 million in twenty years!"

Michael: "Yes, the DOC pays for up to 42 offenders of their 47 population at $135.99 per offender, per day. Annually, that's over 2 million."

Rhonda: "That's a lot of money."

Michael: "It sure is. Remember the news article, when Elk Horn Treatment Center's population was down to 24, leaving 18 of the contracted beds empty? That means those empty beds were causing them to lose over $2,000 per day."

Rhonda: "Yes, that's over $73,000 a month."

Michael: "If ETC's numbers would have remained low, they potentially could have lost over $850,000 in one year. I think we have the answer to why Riverside was shut down. The contract between DOC and private organizations gives the organization the power to tell the DOC what to do, and the legislators gave them that power."

Rhonda: "That's unbelievable. That would tie the hands of the DOC for the length of twenty years!"

Michael: "It seems to me that would also tie the hands of any Governor for the next twenty years as well. That's a lot of power."

Rhonda: "That's just unfathomable."

Michael: "Wait a minute. Look at this on page 7 of 24, it states guaranty of payment by the DOC for 75% of the contracted bed space. The amount of payment is designed to cover ETC's fixed costs."

Rhonda: "So you're telling me that DOC pays ETC for 31 beds, regardless if there is a person in that bed or not?"

Michael: "Yep.... You remember when ETC's population dropped to 24 and the CEO of Boyd Andrews, owner of the Elk Horn Treatment facility, was quoted in the newspaper article saying, 'When the referrals go away, the bills don't go away, the operating costs do not go away. So, it's really harmful on our budget'? According to this, the contract is designed for the DOC to cover ETC's 'fixed' costs. What part of ETC's budget is being affected?"

Rhonda: "It appears that if anything was affected, it was their profits."

Michael: "So, our previous figures of ETC's lost revenue was actually only 11 beds unpaid, not 18. That also means that the DOC was paying for 11 empty bed spaces when ETC was at a population of 24. And like the newspaper article stated, ETC's numbers were down due to referrals to Riverside. The DOC was paying for empty beds at ETC because of our program's success."

Rhonda: "You were right Michael. That's why Riverside was shut down."

Michael: "Let's keep reading. I wonder what else we might find."

Rhonda: "The contract also mandates the treatment center implement prison policies. Like this one right here. *Use of Force MDOC policies 3.1.8*, which is the use of force and restraints, and here is another one *MDOC 3.1.17 Searches and Contraband Control.*

Michael: "Those are policies for the State prison. That 3.1.17 is the policy to implement unclothed searches."

Rhonda: "You mean strip searches? Strip searches are not conducive to treatment and are, in fact, harmful to treatment. Why would they mandate a policy like that in a *treatment* center?"

Michael: "It's a treatment center, but it appears to be operating under policies created for and used in a prison."

Rhonda: "That makes it a prison! Not a treatment center!"

Michael: "I agree. These organizations are disguising a prison with a few licensed professionals on the payroll and a signage out front that says treatment. Don't get me wrong. I know there are good people working in these treatment programs. But I see how policies, contracts, and most of all, money, are getting in the way of these good-hearted people to really and truly help other human beings."

Rhonda: "I worry that most newly licensed professionals will be conditioned to believe in the prison policies and procedures presented to them. I worry they won't feel like they can advocate for better, more effective, treatment methods. I worry they'll believe high recidivism rates are the offender's fault. When in my opinion, the recidivism rates are high due to prolonged treatment governed by prison policies."

Michael: "Right. Prolonged treatment provided at a cost-per-day. It makes me wonder why they'd even want to lower recidivism rates. Seems to me that would put them out of business."

Rhonda: "That's what this seems to be about. It appears to be a business. From a financial perspective, treatment is secondary, if that."

Michael: "Right. When prison policies are running treatment programs and money tied to people being in the programs, the financial profit of it could easily become the priority."

Rhonda: "Where is the incentive to get people out of treatment programs under a contract like this? In fact, from the business perspective, you would want to make treatment programs last as long as possible, even up to nine months."

Michael: "Well, in the case of methamphetamine addictions, they say long-term treatment programs are needed."

Rhonda: "Yes, a 90-day program *is* considered a long-term treatment program.[32] Ask any insurance company. With the exception of community-based sober homes where a person can acclimate to sober living in their own community, 90 days is intimidatingly long."

Michael: "So outside of correctional treatment facilities, programs are considered long at the three-month mark?"

Rhonda: "Yes. Intimidatingly long."

Michael: "I suppose when non-profit or not-for-profit organizations are collecting money for people, per day, they would have an incentive to continue programs lasting three times the normal length of stay."

Rhonda: "Especially when contracts last twenty years."

---

32 https://www.addictioncenter.com/treatment/top-10-drug-treatment-centers/

Several legislators asked the Montana Legislative Audit Committee to conduct a performance audit of the Department of Correction's contracted programs. The audit was released to the public in June of 2020. From the audit work, a determination is made as to whether agencies and programs are accomplishing their purposes, and whether they can do so with greater efficiency and economy.

Performance audits conducted by the legislative audit division are designed to assess state government operations. This audit focused on contract management activity for fiscal years 2016 through 2019. The DOC pays a per diem for offenders placed in the contracted programs. The value of the contracts totaled around $43.9 million in fiscal year 2019.

The audit assessment work identified three risk areas related to contract management, the offender placement process, and the evaluation of the effectiveness of the contracted programs. Subsequently, three objectives were identified to address these risks:

> **Objective #1:** Does the department ensure the requirements of the contracts for community corrections programs are clearly defined, aligned with best practices and are monitored to assure they are met?
>
> **Objective #2:** Does the department ensure offenders are placed in the appropriate contracted community corrections programs according to best practices and department policy?
>
> **Objective #3:** Do contracted community corrections programs affect length of time in or return to the criminal justice system?[33]

---

33 https://leg.mt.gov/lad/audit-reports

Michael and Rhonda reviewed the 47-page legislative audit and found it to validate many of their concerns.

Rhonda: "This audit estimates that the contracted community corrections programs only reduce recidivism by 14%. The average success rate is only 14 %? I can't believe taxpayers are forced to spend millions of dollars for such a low outcome!""

Michael: "The audit reports the DOC does not use offender outcome data to evaluate whether these contracted programs reduce recidivism. Regardless, the 14% rate from the audit committee suggests a recidivism rate of 86%. That's terrible and unacceptable."

Rhonda: "Am I reading this right? It's stating that the DOC paid over $400,000 for empty bed space. Can that really be true? Montana taxpayers paid over $400,000 for no services. What a total waste!"

Michael: "Yah, and I imagine a significant amount of that empty bed space was at a cost due to the referrals to Riverside, which was department owned. The contract stipulation of guaranteed payments by the department for 75% of the contracted bed space, full or not, is a major contributor to that cost. The Montana DOC has no choice. They are bound by contract to send people to these nonprofit private organizations, and when they don't, they pay for empty bed space, which constitutes a waste of state resources."

Rhonda: "You're right! But I believe the department had a choice in the beginning of the contract, and should have never signed a contract that did not include performance or outcome measurements; especially when they sign a contract for the length of twenty years. Montana taxpayers should be outraged!"

Michael: "I agree with you, and as a taxpayer, I am outraged. As a person who values successful treatment, I am outraged. However, I can see that most state officials and the current DOC administration have little to no control now. Many of them have inherited these contracts. Even the current Governor inherited these contracts, and his term is ending soon. So, the next Governor will also inherit these contracts. The amount of power behind these twenty-year contracts is just crazy."

Rhonda: "And the saddest part of all to me is that the department did have an effective program when Riverside was in operation. And because of the pressure to keep those other beds full, Montana will not likely see a difference in rehabilitation or recidivism rates until these contracts have expired."

Michael: "That's right, and this audit reports that when the DOC doesn't assess the effectiveness based on the outcomes of these programs, there is little incentive for contractors to improve outcomes, and it appears there are no penalties to the contractors when offenders do reoffend. Montana communities must continue to endure these contracts for another 7 years in some cases. We can only hope another twenty-year contract won't be approved."

Rhonda: "I would hope that legislators would demand an immediate change in the contracts. These contracts are here to provide treatment and rehabilitation, and currently they have very little guidelines and nothing in their contracts holding accountable to effective treatment. I find that ironic as accountability is drilled into the minds of every person who has been put in prison."

Michael: "I'm struggling to fully understand why this audit was requested by some legislators. I find it peculiar that the data reviews are focused from 2016 to September of 2018. Riverside was shut down September 2018."

Rhonda: "Maybe the shutdown of Riverside provoked the audit, maybe it was something else. I'm just happy that this audit was done and that someone is looking to improve corrections. I wish they would do an audit on every system that works with an oppressed population."

Michael: "The audit interviewed individuals incarcerated in contracted community corrections programs. It looks like the feedback was sporadic as to whether it was effective or not. If I was an incarcerated person being asked if I thought the program which I was currently in was good or bad, I would be very hesitant to answer with a negative report as it could affect how I'm treated for the remainder of my program. They should be talking to people who are not oppressed at the time of questioning. In other words, ask people who have gone through the program, but are not in it at the time of questioning."

Rhonda: "I agree they would get more honest feedback, people who have been incarcerated know the system. They have lived in it. They know they can be referred back into the same facility, just as this audit states. I find this to be utterly flabbergasting! The more we review this audit, the more I believe that contracted treatment providers are another name for extensions of the prisons. It's disgusting, the whole process is disgusting!"

Michael: "That's all they seem to be. Extensions of the prisons, claiming to provide treatment to convince the taxpayers that the money is being spent on something other than building more state prisons. We've said it. Treatment programs implemented under prison policies and procedures are not providing successful treatment, and the recidivism rates prove it.

And look at this! The audit points out what we have been concerned about regarding these contracted organizations feeding themselves through the ability to refer offenders to their own programs. That's a flat-out conflict of interest."

Rhonda: "You bet it is, and the most despairing part of it all, is the people needing treatment are forced to forego effective treatment, or are hoodwinked into believing that the system is there to provide effective treatment."

Our Vision

It continually amazed Michael and Rhonda how challenging, and at times, seemingly impossible it was to implement effective treatment in a correctional setting. They often had long conversations about their vision for justice reform.

Michael: "I long for the day when the Department of Corrections has a truly separate department and/or division for treatment programs and facilities. One entirely separated from the policies and procedures created for a prison and jail environment and culture. When all of the treatment facilities, both owned by and/or privately contracted by the department, have its own unique policies and procedures, solely in support of administering effective treatment, while maintaining a safe environment. We would then be in a better position to reduce recidivism and overcrowding of prisons and jails."

Rhonda: "Right! And it should be implemented at a legislative level and across the board in all 50 states. Also, at the legislative level, they would remove strip searches within all treatment programs. SAMHSA© has invested significant time and money gathering all stakeholders together, and they have formatted the solution. They have released specific guidelines to help institutions implement key components of a best practice. We need legislative members to mandate it into law."

Michael: "Yes. We managed to keep Riverside safe without implementing the strip search. We know this is possible. We would not be re-traumatizing people if a body scanner was implemented, as opposed to making people take their clothes off. We all get body scanned at the airports just to fly anywhere. There is money out there for things like body scanners. We just need legislative members to enforce it. What about treatment programs in state penitentiaries?"

Rhonda: "In my opinion, that's not treatment. All that can really be done in a prison is educate and inform prisoners. It's like calling a strip search an unclothed search, or referring to 'power and control' as 'safety and security'. Giving it a nice name doesn't change what it is. Treatment is not possible with an oppressed population in a prison environment with current prison policies and procedures. I don't care what they call it, it's not treatment."

Michael: "That's similar to giving the housing unit staff of a treatment facility the title correctional counselor, but sending them to correctional officer trainings. The title fits the treatment agenda, but the training is contrary.

We need correctional counselors to manage the housing units of treatment facilities to support the relationship-based rapport. Correctional counselors need their own unique training, separate from the correctional officer prison/jail training. This specialized training would be in support of providing security from a treatment perspective, not a power and control perspective."

Rhonda: "It really boils down to treating people like people, and not as a criminal. If you treat someone like a lesser being, like a criminal, or as if they are behaviorally unstable, that is what you get back, behaviorally unstable actions, criminal actions, attitudes and/or behaviors of resistance."

Michael: "I agree. In addition, our entire justice system needs to stop judging the whole tree based off of a few bad apples. So many policies and procedures are in place in anticipation for the worst-case behavior. Most incarcerated people are being treated as if they are the worst person the system can imagine them to be. By treating them like they are dangerous people, and creating an environment which prepares for dangerous people, the incarcerated person is far more likely to take on that role and act like a dangerous person. By treating them like they are successful, even before they might be, along with creating a therapeutic environment, suggests they are more likely to take on the role of a well-behaved successful person."[34]

Rhonda: "Organizations also need to recognize they limit themselves when they use *only* evidence-based practices. Organizations need to hire, and then trust their teams to make sound decisions, think for themselves, and to make sure the treatment approach they are considering has merit, without boxing themselves into a never-improving treatment approach."

Michael: "Right. How do we expect to grow if we never try anything new? Some organizations consider themselves at the pinnacle of their potential. When I look at the evolutionary progression of an organization, such as the correctional system, I am appalled at how it was treating people 100 years ago, or even 50 years ago. What will they say about us 50 years from now? I can only hope we aren't strip searching in treatment facilities."

---

34 Wittington PhD, Dean. (2016) *Psychologically Informed Environments: Therapeutic Regeneration*. AuthorHouse.

Rhonda: "Well, we both know that neither one of us will be strip searching anyone for the rest of our lifetimes. But, it's not only strip searches, it's that most prison policies and culture interfere with treatment."

Michael: "Right, and I hope one day that treatment is made available on a volunteer basis and not forced, threatened, or presented as an ultimatum. If everyone entering treatment did so at their choice, I believe the need for excessive security measures in treatment facilities would decrease. When a person seeks treatment, they should be viewed as being responsible."

Rhonda: "We've proven that we can decrease excessive security measures in a treatment program. You're right, when a person seeks treatment, it is responsible, and it should be celebrated as such. People should remember how hard it is to come to the realization that your life is out of control and in need of help. That kind of insight is incredibly difficult to integrate."

Michael: "That reminds me of the women who progressed through our program. I wonder how they're all doing?"

Rhonda: "If we had a post-graduate peer-reviewed study done on the program at Riverside, we would know more, not only how the women are doing, but also what is contributing to their success or failure."

Michael: "I saw a few of the women in the news. Unfortunately, some have re-offended."

Rhonda: "I know one woman went back into the system just for being with her boyfriend, who was also on parole. Her boyfriend was sent back to prison as well. Neither of them had committed a crime, they were found kissing each other, that's all they did. I don't understand how probation and parole can realistically expect people to stay away from those they love. Why do they dictate issues of the heart? It will never work because the love connection is too strong. The system needs to recognize this. In 2016, more than 60,000 people were returned to prison for parole violations, not crimes."[35]

Michael: "Even if correctional treatment were to take an evolutionary leap in this direction, it would be necessary for probation and parole to minimize their 'power and control hold' on the people. Providing good treatment is step one, and it should be the first step in not treating them like an inmate. However, we need probation and parole to continue the direction as people re-enter the community."

Rhonda: "Yes, probation officers should be educated on person-centered training and apply that to community supervision."

Michael: "I know we both have criticized the correctional system. And I stand behind it all, but I also understand how the correctional system has become so fear-based. Every policy and procedure are in place to provide some level of safety. And every needed level of safety is to avoid or prevent being liable for the consequence. Our society has blamed the correctional system for every offender who has ever reoffended. It's not fair to blame the correctional system for people making poor choices. If society would stop blaming the correctional system for this, it might allow for a culture of treatment within the correctional system."

Rhonda: "If we stopped assigning blame, judgement or condemnation of people, agencies, or organizations, we would then be in a better mindset to be open to seek solutions. We and every

35 www.prisonpolicy.org

person who have entered Riverside were so blessed be in the mindset of acceptance of people and committed to help them."

Michael: "Yes, however, society has assigned the DOC the responsibility of *fixing* people. Society has wrongfully charged the department with being responsible for people and their behavior outside the prisons. If we task the department with *helping* people after prison sentencing, as opposed to *fixing* them by *controlling* them, then the department could better provide meaningful treatment and supervision to reintegrate people back into the communities successfully."

Evolution of Corrections

Michael: "The correctional organization is continually evolving, as it should be. It would be a mistake for the organization to conclude it has reached a pinnacle of its evolution. It must continue to evolve and mature in its policies, ethics and culture. However, I believe the current system is in its most dangerous and forbidding place during its entire evolution. It's policies and procedures have become locked into a defense of its "safety and security" reasons. Its justification of policies is argued as the only solution to keeping inmates and staff safe. This is a dangerous place for the organization to be because it becomes difficult to further improve its practices, when to do so is argued as 'unsafe.'"

Rhonda: "A great example of that is the difficulty we experienced when trying to reach a consensus to not strip search the residents. Everyone thought we would not be able to maintain a safe environment."

Michael: "Exactly, and look at the correctional system in the 1800's and its use of the pillory and whipping post to enforce prisoner reform. During this era, the use of the pillory was believed to be an appropriate and successful act towards reform. Correctional officers did the whipping because they were ordered to do so under the organization's policy. At some point in time, I believe officers must have felt the act was abusive. But without the power to stop it, they had to partake in the act to maintain their employment. Looking back on this era, it is easy to see it was not a means of reform, but rather a means of abuse."

Rhonda: "Many of our system practices were initially implemented to keep people safe. I believe that when we trust our gut instincts enough to pull back and then look from an objective perspective and change what causes us to feel wrong, we will make improvements. If we would not have done this in the mental health system, we would still be giving many people a lobotomy."

Michael: "In the 1900's, the correctional system moved into inmate labor as the new mainstream reform. Factory prisons were built producing a broad range of finished products. Inmates were forced to work to gain their freedom back. This act of reform began with the intention to provide inmates with trade skills, but quickly manifested into slave labor. This resulted in increased resentment from prisoners, and as a result, they viewed incarceration with even more discontent for the system."[36]

Rhonda: "I see that occurring today. It appears to me that most people coming from incarceration and being placed on probation and parole grow a bitterness toward the correctional system. I believe that if we revamped treatment within corrections, we

36 The American Prison: From the Beginning… A Pictorial History. American Correctional Association. (1983).

could change the feeling setpoint from bitterness to hopefulness, and possibly even trustworthiness."

Michael: "I would add that with good treatment, incarcerated people would gain a newfound respect for the correctional professionals and the organization itself. It's this positive relationship which would support the successful reintegration back into our communities, and therefore reduce recidivism and overcrowding of penitentiaries."

Rhonda: "I agree. It really boils down to seeing people as human, using humanity during conversation and process. We've stated it earlier, if we treat a person like a criminal, how can we expect them not to act like a criminal. People need to believe in themselves and in their ability to be better before they get better. Currently, we give them the message that they are sub-human, non-human, or 'just a criminal', yet expect them to operate their life with perfection. And when they don't, we use an increased display of force to make them succumb. I, too, would have an increased disdain for the system."

Michael: "It seems to me that the war declared on drugs was another knee-jerk reaction to criminal behavior. The first person to use the phrase, 'the war on drugs,' was President Nixon in the late 1970's. When we look at what was happening in the late 1960's, we see civil rights movements and protests of the Vietnam War. It's arguable that the war on drugs was more of a war on people and protesters. President Regan doubled down on the declaration of the war on drugs. Ever since then, police departments have been trained to go to war against American civilians. Of course, this 'war' was not only fought on the streets, it was further ingrained into the justice system and the correctional system.

It didn't take long before the prisons and jails were more overcrowded than ever before. This led to corrections becoming more involved in treatment."

Rhonda: "Yea, it did. However, DOC has little knowledge of *how* to deliver treatment in a manner that is effective for treatment. They know how to deliver treatment about as well as I know *how* to capture and control anyone. The differences from the onset are simply too far apart."

Michael: "Right. And now, we have privatized contractors who have moved in, and in a big way. They are managing prisons, treatment centers, pre-release centers, sanctions and assessment centers. Most of them are listed as non-profit or not-for-profit organizations. Money is being made by providing "bed space". Another word for bed space is human beings. What is it called when people are bought and sold?"

Rhonda: "Slavery. They call that slavery."

Michael: "Their sales pitch is that they can offer lower costs per day. But we should question this for several reasons. How cost effective is the lowest cost per day when contracts last decades? Another concern is if a private organization has a low cost per day, but only moves half the people through the program compared to a program that has a little bit higher cost per day, but provides better treatment in a shorter amount of time, and ultimately reduces recidivism? These contracts are so solid that the privatized organizations have the power to eliminate any competition, including competition from the very department it contracts with. From a business perspective, it's a brilliant move."

Rhonda: "From a treatment perspective, it's insidious. When is treatment, actual treatment, going to be the primary focus? How are we going to measure our success and evaluate our delivery when the twenty-year contract stipulations are more about money, and less about treatment outcomes and recidivism rates?"

Michael: "I hope the next evolutionary leap for corrections is to reform how it is implementing its treatment in privately contracted and department-owned facilities. They must acknowledge the necessary separation between prison cultures and treatment cultures. Privately owned organizations and DOC are in the lucrative exchange of buying and selling human beings with taxpayer money, separating families for long durations and oppressing freedom, all under the mask of providing treatment."

"Don't give up before the miracle."
Resident Testimony

CLOSING

We want our readers to know we don't assume to have all the answers to the world's problems. We have shared our experiences and opinions in hopes to create further dialog around a very complex issue. We are exercising our first amendment right. As stated in our acknowledgment, we have met, and worked with, and know of many hardworking and dedicated people in the correctional and treatment fields. We hope this book will help break down barriers which limit people trying to provide good treatment. We hope to help find the perfect balance in the correctional system's policies and procedures so that human beings in oppressed situations can truly heal. Anytime we, as a society, move in the direction of helping people, as opposed to hurting them, we are moving in the right direction.

> "Put them in prison or invite them to treatment."
>
> "What will society say about us, 100 or even 50 years from now?"
>
> *Michael Johnson*
>
> "I hope society will say great things about our humanity, about our ability to recognize our wrongs and our willingness to correct them."
>
> *Rhonda Champagne*

DEDICATIONS

I dedicate this book to Rhonda Champagne.
Thank you, Rhonda.
Michael Johnson

I dedicate this book to the team at Riverside and the 189 women who entered our facility and believed in themselves.
Rhonda Champagne

TESTIMONIES

Testimonies to Riverside

Submitted by James R. Seymour

The women residents of Riverside came from the dark side of the moon where abuse, neglect, chemicals, family sorrow, and trauma were the only ways of life they really knew. Loss of freedom, health, their "personhood", and death were expected destinations - survival a detour and a rich "quality-existence" in life a mirage. But upon crossing the Boulder treatment center threshold, strong winds of life breathed through them - often for the first time. And with them they brought keen intuitions, the wisdom of hellacious experiences, and work ethics like no others I had ever seen before. I have been in the business of doing therapy for over half a century; and these women - princesses and queens all - came to break bread with their souls. I had never been part of such power and empowerment until Riverside.

The readiness they possessed to shake their souls to the core "and" the setting the incredibly noble, dedicated, and open-minded staff brought to the same altar for this eucharist of change were profound. "Almost-miracles", magic, and the gifts of deep learning were passed around by staff and residents in brimming chalices. My journey as a psychotherapist has taken me to multiple inpatient and outpatient places in several states, but Riverside was the only "stay" where I thrived so fully as student "and" teacher with every fellow employee and literally with every woman who walked through the door. I was honored and - honestly - blessed to be part of this new, needed, and exceptionally successful experiment.

Hope and happiness are usually temporary flirtations with reality, but at Riverside I sensed, heard, and saw the residents of such salty lives become "empresses" who, alas, sniffed the wild possibilities of what the human spirit can do, can become, "and" a self-love they did not know existed. The "Riverside people" - these amazing "scholars of love" - made the environment available for the "Riverside women" to do their growing and evolving with newfound trust and even joy.

That Riverside closed down is more than a mistake. It is a sin with Corrections taking poison hemlock yet again. It was the best experience for many people wherein letting go, loving, moving forward, and where miracles of varying degrees happened for everyone. It was far beyond just a state institution. It was a special place that is a model for how to do it right and treat everyone with the dignity we all deserve.

James R. Seymour, Riverside Licensed Addiction Counselor

* * * * * * * * * *

Reese Dye

There are too many things I wish to say to everyone, to the world, yet that would consist of me writing my own book and that isn't my purpose here. Growing up being sexually, mentally, emotionally, psychically abused by not only the people closed to me, people I thought I could trust, but by honestly anyone I could remember. Being just 5 years old and having my innocents taken away, having no one to talk to, nowhere to go, no one to trust anymore, simply nowhere to run, but yet having so much to run from. Being one of the first 100, actually one of the first 50 girls to go to Riverside was such an incredible experience, it's truly unexplainable. Riverside and the people there gave me something that was awfully taken from me at such a young age. It's been years and the people that created and operated that program had such an impact in my life, made more of a difference than anyone else I had ever met before. They gave me hope, a purpose, a voice again. They gave me back what I had been missing for years, and that was my life. I could spend the rest of my life trying to do something for Riverside, and all of the people, to give them some sort of recognition and appreciation but I feel I would have to spend the rest of my life and that still would never be enough for me. Riverside was filled with hopes and dreams of the women that lost them outside of those walls. Every girl I met there actually wanted to work for the company because everyone was so happy, so amazing, so different then everyone else in this world. I hope that every correctional counselor that I had the honor of meeting & getting to know reads this, because not a day goes by that every morning as I wake up, before I set my feet on the ground, there isn't one of you that I don't thank god or the creator for your existence. I am forever filled with so much love & gratitude for being able to say that I was one of the luckiest women to get to experience the magic that Riverside held, the miracles that became reality in those very walls themselves. This world needs more opportunities like this, it changed my entire perspective and saved my life.

Reese Dye, Riverside Resident

* * * * * * * * * *

Carissa Whitewolf

I was a resident at Riverside Treatment Facility from October 2016 through February 2017. My experience at Riverside was literally life-changing! I have been sober for 3.5 years now and my quality of life is so much more than I could have imagined it could be! I still live in the same town with the same people and the same everyday problems. But thanks to the Riverside program, I now have the tools and the confidence to face those obstacles. Before Riverside, I felt lost and alone, like there was no hope left for me. But the program and the staff did a lot to help rebuild my self-esteem and faith in myself. The most memorable aspect of the program was how they only allowed positivity to reign there. That positivity was the steppingstone to my progress. At Riverside, I was reminded that I was a person worth loving and that I had to love and respect myself. The problems or obstacles that I felt couldn't be overcome, they helped me work through. During my stay, I experienced Halloween, Thanksgiving and Christmas, sober, for the first time in years. I was reminded that these holidays were about gratitude and happiness. It was the first time in a long time I went to bed early on New Year's! All of the staff were amazing and never treated me like I was a criminal. They inspired me to be a better version of myself. They made me feel appreciated after years of feeling less than worthy. Many of them even went out of their way to spend a few moments offering advice and saying goodbye the last night I was there. That went a long way to make me feel like I had been heard and that what they had shared with me during my time at Riverside was genuine. I wasn't just another number, I was number 26 and I am grateful for the staff at Riverside Treatment Facility, the Riverside Treatment Program and, "clouds that touch the mountain, especially in the morning!"

Sincerely,
Carissa Whitewolf, Riverside Resident

* * * * * * * * * *

Ryan Cantrell

I worked as a Correctional Counselor at Riverside Recovery and Re-Entry Program from September 2017 to May 2018. Working as a counselor was a fun and rewarding experience. During my time at the program, I had the opportunity to teach group lessons such as, *Thinkingfor a Change*, *StrengthsFinders*, and *Practicing Positives*. It was interesting learning about theresidents' past experiences and I enjoyed sharing some of my own as well during group discussions. The recreational activities were a blast and the staff were encouraged to play. We played sports like Wall Ball, Softball, and Basketball, and even had some gym time. In some circumstances, I even had the residents exercising on the unit with me. The most rewarding part of the job was counseling the residents through difficult times and watching them develop coping skills throughout their time at the program. Riverside was an exceptional program that employed staff who truly cared about the success of the female residents.

Ryan Cantrell, Riverside Correctional Counselor

* * * * * * * * * *

Hali Devine

How riverside changed me as a person.

When I first came to Riverside, I didn't realize I was lost in my own idea of what I thought I knew about myself. I had no idea who I really even was then. There were so many staff there that spent so much time making sure we had the time and resources to really get to know ourselves. I believe the more you know yourself the more confident you can be, and the level of confidence you have in yourself will impact the amount of negativity you allow in your life. Every night we would have time to say what we were grateful for in that moment. Listening to what others were grateful for really opened my eyes to what I was grateful for without even recognizing it otherwise. The book we worked in with Ms. Champagne was deep. The questions in the book were sometimes hard to answer. But writing them down, knowing they were private and safe was so healing. It was like writing it down to give it away so I didn't have to hold onto it in my own mind anymore and I could finally be free from it all. When I left Riverside, I was confident in myself in a way I had never been before. I spent my entire time there getting to know myself as me, without anyone from my personal life getting involved in my mindset. I grew as a person. I learned me as me. Now I have my children back, I run a multimillion-dollar business, I have purchased my first home, and I am 4.5 years clean from my addiction. I am strength, I am survival, I am confidence, I am me and I don't need anyone's influence to change me. #81 "Confidence isn't walking into a room and comparing yourself to everyone around you, its walking into the room and not having to compare yourself to anyone else in the first place"... be you. be free.

Hali Devine, Riverside Resident

* * * * * * * * * *

Daniel

Riverside and all the staff there helped me tons and since I've been out, I've stayed on the straight path. I have my daughter back, I have a nice house, a job, and I'll be off probation in 2 days!!!! Thank you guys for being awesome and caring people, it's got to take a really caring person to be able to deal with and help out all the ladies you guys have helped out. God bless you both!!!

Daniel, Riverside Resident

* * * * * * * * * *

Jayde Burke

My time at Riverside was what I would say was magical. Literally, the safest place I had ever been to. I remember getting off the transport van and seeing this place. The moment I went through the doors, I could feel the love and compassion. I instantly knew that this was going to be the treatment program that would help me make the change I so desperately needed. The work began immediately. Mentally, physically, and emotionally. The staff there were by far the most patient, understanding, caring, and funny group of "corrections officers" I have ever met. They were all always there for us whenever we needed to talk. But the ladies that were there with me, every single woman I spent time with there were so brave and so strong. We became like sisters. Which brings me to the most powerful moment I remember. You see, I was one of the last remaining girls to graduate before Riverside shut down. The day we received the news all the staff and all the residents were together in a room crying together. We were all devastated in one way or another. I just couldn't believe the impact that those words had on every single one of us. I just know, for me, that every woman or man, incarcerated or not, should experience a facility such as Riverside. There should be more Riversides.

Jayde Burke, Riverside Resident

* * * * * * * * * *

Gina Gonzalez

I was a resident at Riverside from December 2017 to March of 2018. This was the best treatment I've had (I've been to a few). I learned many things there and met some of the most compassionate people, it was great knowing how much the counselors and all the staff genuinely cared about each and every one of us. It was one of the most positive experiences of my life. Thank you, Riverside!

Gina Gonzalez, Riverside Resident #109

* * * * * * * * * *

Matthew Wilson

My time as a Correctional Counselor at Riverside was also where I saw the most professional and personal growth. When I started out there, I had a vague idea that I would he helping incarcerated woman prepare for re-entry. What I discovered in my career is there is the significant impact that trauma has on addictions. The drive and growth you can discover in people when they feel believed in, and the powerful effect it has to allow someone to have an active influence in their treatment. I believe that Riverside changed the lives of every woman who went through our program, and even if they did not leave our program and stay in the community, we certainly left them better equipped to change their lives when they were ready. I am grateful for the growth that I saw, and the impact it had on me.

Matthew Wilson, Riverside Correctional Counselor

* * * * * * * * * *

Charlotte Vondrich

> "Imperfection is beauty, madness is genius, and it is better to be absolutely ridiculous than absolutely boring." ~ Marilyn Monroe

My name is Charlotte and I went to Riverside from November2017 to February2018. I was your typical bad attitude, "you can't teach me anything" addict. Boy, was I wrong. The family bond between the staff there and the personal attention they gave me helped me realize in my muddled world of addiction, I wasn't alone. I lashed out and acted out many times while I was there. They didn't just throw me in a room and shut the door. They came and taught me right from wrong, shared their own life stories, and reminded me that I was enough. Ms. Champagne was amazing!! I was so filled with self-hate that many times she just said to me, "why do you hate this wonderful person so much?" I never understood how amazing I was until she opened my eyes. I am over two years into recovery from drugs and four years recovered from a ten-year long domestically violent marriage. I have a beautiful healthy relationship with my children and a very respectful man that loves ME. Riverside showed me how to love myself and how to be okay with the wrongs I have made in my life. Thank you.

Charlotte Vondrich, Riverside Resident #105

* * * * * * * * * *

Matthew H. Hoffman

Wow, wow, wow! This book is a MUST read for EVERYONE! Addiction is an incredibly destructive force in our world today and people like Michael and Rhonda are the ones who are going to start a movement in the treatment world. I am a recovering addict who has been through every State facilitated treatment program you can think of. Although I learned much while in these programs, I still came out feeling broken, or just not quite whole. The story of the two sides (trauma therapy and DOC security) coming together in unity to love those who were at their lowest is heartwarming and powerful. You are sure to enjoy the witty banter between the Therapist and Lieutenant as they battle out their differences before coming to a solution for all. The ending will have you fired up and ready to stand firm for this cause of Correcting Treatment in Corrections.

Matthew H. Hoffman, Peer Support

* * * * * * * * * *

Alyssa Allen

I just got the news about Riverside and am heartbroken. I'm so happy I was sent to your facility over any other in Montana. Riverside made me who I am today: a mother, fiancé, daughter, sister & friend. I have been sober for 3 years now. I never thought I'd be where I am now... buying a house, starting my own business & being the best mother I can be! Riverside made me feel like I had a chance and that my life was worth more. Thanks to all of you who cared endlessly for all of us women trying to survive!

Alyssa Allen, Riverside resident

* * * * * * * * * *

Anonymous

I wish to commend my coworkers of Riverside. An absolutely amazing group of caring, compassionate & professional people. Who came together and bonded through trainings, meetings, at times arguments and tense debates, but always empathic listening & respectful compromise. Staff of every positional title played an equally important role in creating a safe, therapeutic, accountable and healing environment for women inside the justice system. All staff ensured an atmosphere where women dealing with significant emotional trauma could start to experience self-value, confidence and self-forgiveness so they may give themselves permission to live a healthier life. While no program is perfect, this was a place where incredible transformations were possible and happened through a trauma informed and trauma responsive platform.

The residents of Riverside deserve acknowledgment for each of their unique personal journeys. They did the hard and deeply personal work of learning to trust the program, developing healthy relationships & boundaries and when appropriate "letting go..." Their personal struggles & triumphs taught us so much about the human spirit and it was a privilege to be witness to their transformation & personal victories.

Anonymous

* * * * * * * * * *

Chantel Cooper

Riverside helped me in so many ways. I never knew that trauma was a part of our problems...a big part. I went there thinking, "no way". My trauma was as little as my parents splitting up when I was 13, or my ex-boyfriend beating me till I was black and blue. I sat there in Rhonda Champagne's class and listened to so many people's stories and talking about my own, some stories mine could never compare to. And crying with those who told their heartbreaking stories and them crying with me to mine CHANGED MY LIFE. I never felt so much love then I did when I was sitting in that room with those ladies. The staff at Riverside had so much love for us and helped us in any way that they could. I have been through so many treatment centers and institutions. But without a doubt, Riverside was the best one. I felt loved, I never had to worry about being thrown in a cold room by myself with food being shoved through the cuff port, or a male or female officer coming in and strip searching us "because they felt like it," like they had a reasonable cause or something. I feel like all DOC treatments need the trauma setting because the way we are treated in those other DOC treatments is sometimes worse than the way we were treated on the streets, and who's that going to change??? Today, I am 2 years and 3 months clean. Riverside showed me how to love myself and pick myself back up again even if I did fall.

Chantel Cooper, Riverside Resident

* * * * * * * * * *

Nicole Smith

My name is Nicole Smith-Music (Jones now). I was attending Riverside when it closed down, and what a sad day that was. If there is one thing I could say about Riverside, it would be that I never thought I would see the day a room full of felons cried when a D.O.C facility was closing. They cried because the system has failed yet again, and it's heartbreaking that no other addict or trauma victim will ever get to receive that help. Riverside was magic; this tiny facility radiated an unbelievable amount of hope, which for the previous 2 years of lock-up before that, was lost for me. Riverside was a game changer. It was so nice to feel like a human again and treated like I was just another person, not a lowlife. At Riverside, I was more than just my rap sheet. I was me again, and that little encounter of kindness and the different setting, rather than your usual facility, changed my life completely. Riverside prepared me and healed me in order for my future to really begin. Riverside was a blessing for me and I'm sad it is gone.

Sincerely,
Nicole Smith-Music, Riverside Resident

* * * * * * * * * *

Anonymous

During the time I spent with the Riverside Recovery Program, I was given the once-in-a-lifetime chance to see an amazing one-of-a-kind program as implemented by your staff, the wonderful Ms. Champagne, and you, yourself (Lt. Michael Johnson). It was incredible to see the effect a trauma-informed, and recovery-focused program can have on a person. Working with the residents, hearing people open up in groups and during one-to-one counseling sessions and taking part in a program that benefited people for the better will always hold a place in my heart. There are no words to express how sad it is that this program was shut down. The residents who in the final days were deprived of the full program, any future residents that may have benefited from the unique and kind approach to recovery that Riverside could have shown them, and the State of Montana as a whole, have truly lost something great. #BringBackRiverside

Anonymous, Riverside Correctional Counselor

* * * * * * * * * *

Taisha

My name is Taisha and I was at Riverside from September 11, 2017 to December 13, of 2017. I got arrested on May 1 of 2017 and part of my sentencing was I had to go to a treatment program. I researched a couple of different places before I put my application in to Riverside. I knew that with my drug addiction it was going to take more than just a 28-day treatment center. I heard about Riverside when I was in jail. I did some research on it and found out that they not only treated the addiction, they bring the trauma from your past to the light and helped you with working through it. That was something that I needed, and I knew it. The staff at Riverside, especially Ms. Champagne, helped me through a lot of issues that I had. Ms. Champagne really helped me realize that I am worth being alive, that I am worth having the love of my family, and that I really do love myself. Since my stay at Riverside, I have moved to Nebraska and I am now in college doing everything that I didn't even think was possible. There are not enough words to express what Mr. Johnson, Ms. Champagne, and all of the other staff members have done for me. I know for a fact that if it would have been any other treatment facility, I would be back on drugs, if not in prison by now.

"I am pretty, but I am not beautiful.
I am good, but I am not an angel.
I sin, but I am not the devil."

Taisha, Riverside Resident

* * * * * * * * * *

Michael Johnson

Working at Riverside and learning what it means to be trauma informed changed my life. In the beginning, I believed trauma was only related to events such as combat PTSD or severe abuse. I learned trauma takes on many forms and influences people on many levels. Trauma cannot be measured from one person to another. It's affects are personal and can only be diagnosed by the individual. At Riverside, I witnessed everyday people suffer the effects of the trauma they have endured. I saw how their trauma can directly and indirectly be the root cause of their addictions and criminal behavior. But the truth is, although I learned of trauma and what it can do to a person's life, I never really understood it fully until Riverside was shut down. It was during this time I divorced from my marriage, lost custody of my second child, lost my job, fell into addiction yet again and I even committed a crime. More than one. Despite all I knew of trauma I still wasn't able to cope appropriately. It all just seemed to happen so fast. I now, fully understand the effects of trauma. Good people can make bad choices when their trauma is not addressed appropriately through uplifting and positive treatment.

Our correctional treatment systems spend far too much effort on breaking people down who are already broken. Trauma treatment is about supporting and teaching people to become powerful and confident. This is how people change their behavior and their lives.

I am so proud of all the women I met in the Riverside program. They are truly the bravest, strongest and most powerful people I have ever met.

Michael Johnson, Lieutenant

* * * * * * * * * *

Dani Jo Kennary

What Riverside did to my life? It did everything! If I could explain Riverside in one word..."Heaven". I was always trying to figure out who I was and where I belonged my whole life. Going into Riverside, I was a follower trying to fit in. And by the end of it, I was a leader. I watched a very close person to me kill himself while I was sitting in the car with him. That was my rock bottom. That's when I knew I needed to change. Without Riverside, the people, and the trauma treatment, I would not be as successful as I am today. Getting into Riverside, I never acknowledged the things that happened to me, like the rape and molestation. It wasn't until I began to talk about it that I was able to realize I had been hanging on to these traumas in my life.

Today, I have over three years clean and sober. I have a nine-month-old daughter. I have confidence and a drive to live a better life. I have never been to a DOC facility like Riverside. Riverside is all about positivity. And if you don't want to talk about something, you don't have to. I have a life that I never could have imagined, and it might not mean much to some people but to me, it is everything and more. I credit this to my higher power, trauma treatment, and all the staff who worked at Riverside.

Dani Jo Kennary, Riverside Resident

* * * * * * * * * *

Riverside Resident

After my son was killed in 2015, I hit rock bottom. Homeless, robbed, trafficked, hospitalized, I had lost everything, and I didn't want to change. In jail I decided, I wanted sobriety, but was discouraged to hear experiences of women who had gone to treatment. I told my story to a woman who looked at getting me into Riverside. I was accepted and relieved. I hoped this place wouldn't re-traumatize me like other facilities I heard of. When I arrived, I felt a sense of safety and hope which I'd never felt before. I was treated with compassion, kindness and never re-traumatized. The things I loved the most were binary beat meditations, vagus nerve work, our specific strengths and Law of Attraction. Ms. Champagne taught me that I have the power to do anything. Her techniques helped me so much that I study it daily. Her intention was to help people heal the trauma which would help the addiction. My life after graduating looks 100% different and gets better every day. I get to be a loving, attentive mom to my redhead called Todd. I study success principles daily with mentor Bob Proctor. I own my own company and am integrated partner at 'Food for The Soul'. I have a car, home and family. I dream of the things I'm doing with my future. I've been told that I inspire people with what I've overcome. This wouldn't be possible without Riverside. THIS is the place that, not only confronts the root (trauma), and the weed (addiction), but also provides soil for more desirable growth. I'm so grateful for the things I learned at Riverside because I know that I wouldn't be where I am without someone reminding me that I'm worthy.

Riverside Resident

* * * * * * * * * *

Lea Wetzel

When I got to Riverside, I had just lost my best friend and number one support, my dad. My one and only sibling, my brother, had lost his battle with this disease while I was in prison back in 2013, and I never got to go to the services to say goodbye. Two years before getting to Riverside, I was a victim of someone else's sick hustle, and told I was very lucky to be alive by the investigating officer because he knew the whole story already. While at that time, I continued to struggle with processing it all from the brain damage. I survived being kidnapped, raped, and almost beaten to death. The part that was the most traumatizing to me was, that it was the people that I called friends who set me up. I had been a victim to many negative obstacles throughout my life, even back in my childhood I dealt with mental, physical, and sexual trauma. I had a very traumatizing experience in MSWP as well, and because of my continuing downward spiral of a lifestyle, I had become almost immune to the wrongs that would occur throughout my stays under the Department of Corrections.

Here is the reality of showing a human that they are human beings and deserve to be treated as such. It's been 28 months, and I'm still sober. I graduated Drug Court and I worked a perfect program while in it, so my record with them was expunged. I have custody of my two beautiful children after 9 years of not having them. I got my license back, and I drive a decent SUV. I was asked by Drug Court to assist with Zoom Meetings on Thursdays, so I'm getting ready to do that soon. I work at a treatment center here where I live, and my boss is the counselor I had before I went to Riverside. She also paid my room and board for me so that I could take the training, Peer Support 101, because of her faith and unconditional love for me. I passed my test and am in the middle of getting certified with the state. I was able to face my offender at his change of plea hearing. He's getting 40 yrs., and I was able to get my voice back. Now I'm involved with empowering others who don't quite have their voices back, and supporting them until they do, and after. I did end up getting a few ailments from the incident, and it does include a TBI, and vision impairment. The difference is, I choose to deal with my issues by staying in counseling, I'm sponsored in a very well-known 12-step program. I meditate, because while being taught how to at Riverside, I was able to make peace with my faults to my brother and dad. I could be better at the working out part of it, but the thing is, I was educated on how to care for myself in multiple aspects including routines, cleaning, cooking, and earning money while I was there. I keep myself surrounded by like people, people that have the same thing in common with me. They're going places. I helped develop a Native Program with a very close friend and we are getting ready to launch here next month. I learned to put myself first or I'm no good to the ones I love. Ms. Champagne taught us all that we need to allow the little girls in us who were hurt out, and allow them to feel that they are safe now. That if we are balanced, including spiritually, mentally, and physically, then we have a better chance at beating the pants off this disease. I found my higher power there. I found my Creator again, but of my own understanding. I was able to go whatever way I wanted to with my spirituality, but I lead very courageously with a great team. The Riverside team that actually cared and took the time to listen, counsel, and have fun with us. They showed me that I mattered, and that I didn't have to own that enormous bag of 'no good' I showed up with at the front door. I pass all that wisdom I was given to not only my children, my clients, fellow human beings, and my boss. We are huge on articulating what works. I think back and it was like a dream, because it's all gone now, and it's not fair to those who didn't get to experience it and who need it. I truly believe if we had these all over for men, women, and children, they would fully benefit hugely like myself, and many others. I'm a living testimony that it works, and I'll continue to fight for what is right until the day I die. Because I realized that my purpose is to fight for those who cannot fight for themselves, because I was one once, before the Riverside Family fought for me.

Lea Wetzel, Riverside Resident

* * * * * * * * * *

Mel Martinez

Picture this, a young girl in a reform school, then going to jail and living most of her adult life in correctional facilities. That girl was me, a 52-year-old recovering addict. While locked up in one of those facilities, I never learned my lesson and always felt ashamed of my situation. After my son shot and killed a man, I relapsed again and was sent to a treatment facility that changed my life.

When Riverside Trauma Therapy Treatment Center picked me up, I felt kindness from the staff immediately. I was actually called Melanie and quickly found out that I belonged in this type of treatment program. There were good days and bad days, as to be expected, but the staff at Riverside taught me self-worth and it was then that I realized that I was more than just a number. Ms. Champagne, my trauma therapist, made me realize that I had a reason to live and fight for.

STRENGTHSFINDER 2.0, written by Tom Rath explains, "We were tired of living in a world that revolved around fixing our weaknesses. Society's relentless focus on people's shortcomings had turned into a global obsession. What's more, we had discovered that people have several times more potential for growth when they invest energy in developing strengths instead of correcting their deficiencies." This quote taught me that people thrive on positive reinforcement, and that negative responses can cause you to have negative actions. After taking the test provided with this book, I found that my top 5 strengths were adaptability, belief, deliberative, empathy, and restorative.

After spending 4 ½ months at Riverside, I found that I did not want to leave. I felt at home and believed that I could be thought of as an actual human being. I would not have made it this far without the love and communication with my family, for the first time in 12 years. I also got to start spending time with my 13-year-old granddaughter. I am currently enrolled in school at Post University, hoping to get my Business degree. These are just some of the things I have gained with positive reinforcement while in a drug treatment program. Nobody can be as hard on you as yourself.

Riverside really helped me, and I know that it can help others as well. Before it closed its doors, I was hoping that my son could experience what I had gone through. Not only did Riverside give me the courage I needed to move on in life, it also gave me the skills I needed to make it in the world today. Thank you, Riverside, for showing me how to better myself without making me feel like a criminal. Thank you, Ms. Champagne, for helping me to see the real me. Lastly, thank you to my friends and family who have supported me through all of my inconsistencies and have made me happier in life.

Mel Martinez, Riverside Resident

* * * * * * * * * *

B. Smith

The Riverside trauma-informed program changed me as a person. It was a program that if you bought into it, you bought into the idea of helping yourself improve as a human being and move forward. Everything was a choice and a choice that you got to make. As a correctional counselor, I felt that the program helped every woman that entered it, to some degree. And the ones that put in the hard work and effort, changed their lives forever because of it. Just ask them, they will tell you, I promise. I never thought I'd find myself enjoying going to work every day wanting to be there. Helping people and seeing the results of your hard work is a

great accomplishment, and that's what we did. You take the good with the bad and you make it the best it can be in the moment. My favorite thing about the program was playing wall ball and baseball with my coworkers and the residents, laughing and having fun. It was a great place to be in my life and if it ever came back, I would be the first one to say I'm in!!
B. Smith, Riverside Correctional Counselor

* * * * * * * * * *

Stella Marie Freaux

My name is Stella Marie Ereaux. I was 42 years old when I was accepted into the Riverside Trauma Recovery Reentry Program. Upon arriving there, I was a mess. I was broken, confused, full of heartache, and pain. I was letting myself be a victim, especially after I became an orphan. When I was in Riverside, I learned how to love myself. The staff, which consisted of mainly male officers, treated us women with the utmost respect. We were treated as equals and not just a number, something you don't see within the Department of Corrections. At Riverside, we were not stripped searched, we did not have to squat and cough, bend over and spread our cheeks. We were not dehumanized in any way shape or form. It was Riverside where I found myself, the one who was lost. I have been able to forgive myself as well as the people that have hurt and betrayed me. Riverside taught me how to deal with my trauma, and for that, I am extremely grateful that I was one of the lucky ones chosen to go there!! The DOC needs to bring it back, they need one for both men and women. If there were more programs in the Department of Corrections that focused on those kinds of traumas, it would bring the relapse rate down. I am one of the first 100 women to complete the program.

Thank you.
Stella M Ereaux, Riverside Resident

* * * * * * * * * *

Tiadora White

My name is Tiadora White and here is my testimony about my experience at Riverside Correctional Facility. All of my life I have struggled with trauma and substance abuse. To be short, I was dealt a bad set of cards in life. I was never taught skills to cope or deal with my issues and I handled them the only way I knew how. I self-medicated, which in turn led me down a life path of trouble. I was never a bad person, I just made bad decisions. Where did that lead me? Losing everything, homeless, trouble with the law, short stints in mental health facilities. It was a never-ending cycle that I was born into and could not get away from! But I was not always like this. I grew up on the Fort Peck Indian Reservation and I witnessed my childhood boyfriend of 5 years commit suicide in front of me, at the age of 17. Without any social skills or coping mechanisms, I fell into a dark hole that lasted almost 8 years, where I ended at Riverside. With this being my first serious offense, I thank the Lord that I was fortunate and blessed enough for my first DOC charge to be served there. Of course, I am not proud of the mistakes I have made. But Riverside truly saved my life. Riverside did something for me that no one had ever done before. The amazing people there treated me like a person and not just another DOC number. Instead of tearing me down and treating me like an animal, they helped me to see my self-worth and they helped me to get to the root of all my troubles. Instead of beating substance abuse workbooks down my throat, we did life-changing ceremonies and group activities that helped me to find closure from the terrible things I have witnessed and been through in my lifetime. They helped me deal with all the skeletons in my closet that have been haunting me and helping to steer my decision-making. I can honestly say that going to Riverside was the best thing that happened to me in my life thus far. Society today expects offenders to get out and not reoffend when all they do is lock them in a room and then never address the reason why the crime was committed in the first place. And no, it's not always just because a junkie needs a fix. Almost always there is a dark seeded trauma that has started everything. America has one of the highest incarceration rates and one of the highest reoffend rates. Obviously, what penitentiary and law officers are doing is not working. Riverside wanted to make a change in the way they treat an offender. All positivity and self-growth to help change your thinking. And I 100% agree with them. I can think of a million reasons why I'm so thankful for Riverside, but just to name a few, I have become healthier spiritually, physically and mentally. I am not perfect, but because of them, I was able to learn new skills to deal with what this hard life can throw at me. Three years later, I am off paper, a mother of a beautiful 2-year-old, employed and free! Finally, free from the dark oppressive hole I had been stuck in for so long. And I thank God for that. Bring back Riverside and you'll bring back a change. Thank you.

Tiadora White, Riverside Resident

* * * * * * * * * *

June Rae McDonald

STRENGTH. That is what I learned I had and what would get me through life (amongst a few other things, like love and patience). But strength is such a profound thing to believe in.

I know that throughout my life, I used to hide behind "tough," "cold," and "indifferent". I was just holding onto pain, hurt, anger, and sadness. But strength was something that I never thought that I had, and I didn't know how to use it, even if I did.

So, I can't tell you exactly what my 1 strength was without digging out my book, but I can tell you that I have used quite a few of my strengths while at Riverside, as well as now.

While at Riverside, my strength led me to my truth. The truth about how my life was and how I was perceiving it to be, are two totally different realities. Acceptance of the truth was probably the hardest part. No more hiding behind alcohol and lies to myself and others. If I was going to make it, I was going to always have to know what my REALITY was. I have to know what my obstacles are. I needed a plan for most everything. But if I stayed in reality, I could find the strength (and what kind of strength) to use to move around the obstacles.

Life has not been perfect for me. I fell. I got back up and pulled it together. I might have to do that a lot for the rest of my life, but I will never just quit.

Strength is my savior.

I was fortunate to have been a resident at Riverside. I met so many talented and caring staff that I almost couldn't believe it! I took a lot out of that program and I prove it every day. I am fully employed at a job I love and I can honestly communicate with my family, I can be honest with myself. I don't have to fight for a good life anymore. I take it bit by bit, do what I can and have dreams. I continue with therapy, I discharged my parole, I have savings in the bank.

Strength brought me home.
June Rae McDonald, Riverside Resident

* * * * * * * * * *

Raelene Evans

My name is Raelene Evans, formally known as inmate number 3077907. I was counted, I was classified, and I was remanded to the DOC system. Being issued a number like this is definitely not something people should be proud of. I find pride in it though because it was something that helped me to become the person that I am today. It took me a long time to realize that and to be grateful for my past. When you are given one of these numbers though, you were stripped of who you are. The only face you have is the photo taken known as your mug shot. When these "photos" are taken, most people are hopeless and broken, and have hit the bottom. The only thing we are known for at the time, was the crimes that we have committed.

I had already done a substantial period of jail time a few months at a pre-release facility and a lengthy treatment program. I only made it a few months in pre-release, and I was sent back to jail with the recommendation of attending and completing the Riverside Reentry Program. I was given a vague description of the program by an internal probation and parole officer. The understanding that I had was that it was a trauma-based program. I filled out the application, signed my name, and carried on with the assumption that it was just going to be the same old facility. My story was riddled with trauma and I had already completed another treatment program. So, I figured jumping through the hoops and completing my necessary sentence would be something that I would just grin and bear about and get through it. The moment I got off the transport vehicle outside of Riverside doors, I knew this was a different place. Upon entering, I was not strip searched, which was something that was extra dehumanizing for me. As previously mentioned, trauma was something that was prominent in my life, including sexual trauma. When you're placed in a situation that brings up memories like that, it is called re-traumatization. However, the staff was warm and welcoming. We started the paperwork and I began learning the rules and procedures of the facility. Low and behold, I soon became aware that this definitely was not the same old treatment facility I've become used to. Trauma was actually going to be addressed. We still had rules, guidelines, and procedures that followed the DOC mandate. But the objection of the program was to resolve trauma-based issues, finding healing, and helping inmates be more prepared for the outside world, and to becoming productive members of society was the goal. In a few short days, I will have three years sober. The tools and techniques that I learned at the Riverside Reentry Program are undeniably tools that have helped me to become all of the things I've needed and wanted to be. My ability to establish healthy relationships, healthy communication, and to be a successful sober human being got better every day. And I owe a great deal of that to the staff at Riverside. It is absolutely amazing the transformation that I saw within myself and countless girls before and after me. People that not only we ourselves, but the system deemed hopeless. How many times do people say we would never be able to make it? That we would continually circle through the system until one day the trauma or the disease, or whatever struggles we were facing, would take us to the grave. I stand here today to prove all of those theories wrong. Michael Johnson took on the task that would seem to some as impossible. In coordination with the other members of his staff, they made the impossible a reality. We are not all hopeless, there is a hope that shines brighter than the sun. There is a way for us to not only recover, but to become better people. I found this hope and this truth while being in Riverside. I would like to give an unmeasurable thank you to Mr. Johnson, Miss Champagne, Mr. Seymour and the rest of the Riverside staff. Thank you for believing in me, thank you for helping me to grow. Thank you for showing me what bravery actually means. Thank you for helping me get my daughter back and being the mother that she deserves to have. Thank you for allowing me to be a mother to a beautiful baby boy who never has to know me through my addiction. And thank you for going above and beyond your call of service.

Raelene Evans, Riverside Resident

* * * * * * * * * *

Rhonda Champagne

I entered Riverside not knowing exactly how or why I got there. The place felt heavy and gray. In fact, for days I did not see any color other than grey. When I arrived, I felt a contrasting combination of fear, anxiety/excitement, hopelessness, and hope.

I expected to be met by people with control and power issues and instead was met by people who were open minded and had a sense of fairness. I also expected to be met with mean spirited and judgmental officers. Again, I was met by people who were seeking betterment. When Riversides correctional counselors met and spoke with women, they did it non-judgmental with an open-minded fairness. These correctional counselors knew that they didn't have to be a therapist to be therapeutic. I am forever grateful for each one of them.

Riverside changed my life. It opened my eyes to the realization that we can create phenomenal change when we believe we can. It also taught me to check my preconceived judgements about others and to be open to relating with the humaneness of other humans.

Riverside was incredibly important to me in so many ways. I learned the value of my often taken for granted life. I learned the value of the person behind the uniform. I learned the value of sharing experiences no matter how hard it was. I learned the value of what my spirit is capable of. Today my world is full of many awe inspiring colors.

With much love and gratitude,
Ms. Champagne, Trauma Therapist

* * * * * * * * * *

Jeanine Ford

I have been blessed repeatedly in my nursing career, but as I move closer to my retirement date, I take time to reflect on some of those special moments with special people. My time as "the-nurse" for the incarcerated women at the Riverside program within the Montana system rises to the top of my gratitude list. Decisions made above our pay grade limited the length of time the program was open, but as a professional nurse and tax-paying citizen, I believe with all my heart and fiscal experience that a trauma informed professional staff and trauma responsive programming for rehabilitation is most cost effective for the participant and public, alike. Being able to treat those in need *holistically* through trauma-responsive programming is not only the most humane means of assisting these individuals but provides the needed footing back into productive lives, where they want to be, and keeping them there, long term. And it certainly provided me the opportunity to deliver the best nursing care of my career, and I hope and pray for the day another program like this is implemented in our great State. Though a paradigm shift for some institutionalized systems, I believe a great new world would shine if this programming was implemented throughout the correctional world.

Jeanine A, Ford Riverside Nurse, RN, BA

* * * * * * * * * *

Josh Wigen

As I think back on my time at Riverside, what I am most proud of is being a part of a staff that invested in the lives of women who were broken. Broken by life and their own choices. The men and women I worked with treated each and every one of the women with respect and dignity, which in turn allowed the women to realize that there was more to each one of them than their trauma and their mistakes. Each woman I came into contact with had value and purpose. I'm proud to say I served with an entire staff of people who looked beyond the transgressions and saw the person underneath. It was truly magical to work at a facility that saw the women not for what they were, but what they could become. I've never in my life been around another group of people who looked beyond the brokenness and saw possibility. When the women saw that the staff recognized possibility in them, they then gave themselves permission to see, and more than that, to hope for that very possibility within themselves. To me it was Camelot, a place that dared to dream of a better world for those who were there and the audacity to believe it was truly possible.

Josh Wigen Riverside Fitness and Education Teacher

REFERENCES

https://www.addictioncenter.com/treatment/top-10-drug-treatment-centers/

Applied Psychology: *Health and Wellbeing* (2011). https://iaap-journals.onlinelibrary.wiley.com

Bernstein, Rebecca. (2016) *The Mind and Mental Health: How Stress Affects the Brain*. Touro University Worldwide. www.tuw.edu/health/how-stress-affects-the-brain./

https://www.boydandrew.com/services/elkhorn/

Common therapy approaches to help the healing process of trauma. (2011) https://www.google.com/search?q=trauma+techniques+therapy&o-q=trauma+techni&aqs=chrome.5.0j69i57j0l6.9886j0j7&sourceid=-chrome&ie=UTF-8

https://cor.mt.gov/Portals/104/Resources/Contracts/Boyd%20Andrew%2007-016-ACCD%20thru%20Amend%205.pdf?ver=2020-01-29-114505-933

Covington, PhD, Stephanie S. (2018) *Moving from Trauma-Informed to Trauma-Responsive*. Hazelden Publishing. https://www.hazelden.org/store/item/520203?Moving-from-Trauma-Informed-to-Trauma-Responsive

Emmons, Robert, a researcher on gratitude, states "Gratitude reduces a multitude of toxic emotions. Gratitude enhances empathy and reduces aggression."

https://eocinstitute.org/meditation/141-benefits-of-meditation/

https://www.essentialed.com/students/hiset-academy?gclid=EAIaIQob-ChMI8b_G4d6E6gIVEB-tBh2uwghWEAAYASAAEgJHvvD_BwE

Highschool Equivalency Test (HISET)® https://www.google.com/search?q=HISET&rlz=1C1GCEA_enUS828US846&oq=HISET&aqs=-chrome..69i57j0l7.3716j0j7&sourceid=chrome&ie=UTF-8

Journal of Applied Sport Psychology (2014). https://www.tandfonline.com

Kleinman, E. M., Adams, L. M., Kashdan. T. B., & Riskind, J. H. (2013). Grateful Individuals Are Not Suicidal. *Personality and Individual Differences*, 55(5), 595-599. https://www.sciencedirect.com/science/article/abs/pii/S019188691300192X

https://leg.mt.gov/lad/audit-reports

Matheson, Flora I. (2012) *Implications of Trauma among Male and Female Offenders*. Ontario, Canada. https://www.mdpi.com/1660-4601/9/1/97

https://www.mtacdl.org/attachments/CPE/Chico_2015/5_CAmbrose DOCComProg.pdf

McDermott, Ted. "'*A Big Break in the Program': Elkhorn Treatment Center Population Drops by Nearly Half*." Montana Standard. June 19, 2018. https://mtstandard.com/news/local/a-big-break-in-the-program-elkhorn-treatment-center-population-drops-by-nearly-half/article_58955590-f841-50ac-82c0-8df269e9d536.html

https://outdoor-fit.com/mental-health-benefits-exercise-prison

Pipher, Mary. (2006). *Writing to Change the World.* Penguin Group (Amazon indicates that the publisher is Riverhead Books)

https://positivepsychology.com/what-is-positive-psychology-definition/

Practicing Positive Worksheets (2009). https://www.google.com/search?q=practicing+positive+worksheets&rlz=1C1GCEA_enUS828US846&oq=practicing+positive+worksheets&aqs=-chrome..69i57.10824j1j7&sourceid=chrome&ie=UTF-8

www.prisonpolicy.org

Rath, Tom. (2007). *StrengthsFinder 2.0.* Gallup Press https://www.amazon.com/StrengthsFinder-2-0-Tom-Rath/dp/159562015X

Starecheski, Laura. (2015) *Take the ACE Quiz – And Learn What It Does and Doesn't Mean.* https://www.npr.org/sections/health-shots/2015/03/02/387007941/take-the-ace-quiz-and-learn-what-it-does-and-doesnt-mean

Substance Abuse and Mental Health Services Administration (SAMHSA)©

https://www.samhsa.gov

The American Prison: From the Beginning… A Pictorial History. American Correctional Association. (1983).

The Journal of Personality and Social Psychology (2017). https://psycnet.apa.org

The Sentencing Project. (2017). *Research and Advocacy and Reform* www.Sentencingproject.org/criminal-justice-facts/

Top Ten Offenses for Male and Female Offenders in Montana (2019). https://cor.mt.gov/Portals/104/Resources/Reports/2019biennialreport.pdf

Trauma Informed Oregon. (2010) *What is Trauma Informed Care?* https://traumainformedoregon.org/wp-content/uploads/2016/01/What-is-Trauma-Informed-Care.pdf

Walden University (2013-2014). *5 Mental Benefits of Exercise.* https://www.waldenu.edu/online-bachelors-programs/bs-in-psychology/resource/five-mental-benefits-of-exercise

Wittington PhD, Dean. (2016) *Psychologically Informed Environments: Therapeutic Regeneration.* AuthorHouse. https://books.google.com/books?id=9_yRDQAAQBAJ&pg=PT82&lpg=PT82&dq=-authoritative+command+brings+about+negative+behavior&-source=bl&ots=BxVhYYOhA0&sig=ACfU3U2S8xTozQIkaB-SInT3ZzRe5GpGA&hl=en&sa=X&ved=2ahUKEwj3vJuHqsDpA-hUjIDQIHZgND0YQ6AEwAHoECAgQAQ#v=onepage&q=authoritative%20command%20brings%20about%20negative%20behavior&f=false

Ziegler, Erin Holaday. *Gratitude as an Antidote to Aggression* (2011). University of Kentucky https://psychology.as.uky.edu/gratitude-antidote-aggression